HYDROPONICS

The Essential Guide to Learn Everything About a Hydroponic Gardening System and How to Easily DIY to Produce Homegrown Fresh and Healthy Vegetables, Herbs, and Fruits

Mark Bennett

© Copyright 2020 by Mark Bennett. All right reserved.

The work contained herein has been produced with the intent to provide relevant knowledge and information on the topic on the topic described in the title for entertainment purposes only. While the author has gone to every extent to furnish up to date and true information, no claims can be made as to its accuracy or validity as the author has made no claims to be an expert on this topic. Notwithstanding, the reader is asked to do their own research and consult any subject matter experts they deem necessary to ensure the quality and accuracy of the material presented herein.

This statement is legally binding as deemed by the Committee of Publishers Association and the American Bar Association for the territory of the United States. Other jurisdictions may apply their own legal statutes. Any reproduction, transmission, or copying of this material contained in this work without the express written consent of the copyright holder shall be deemed as a copyright violation as per the current legislation in force on the date of publishing and subsequent time thereafter. All additional works derived from this material may be claimed by the holder of this copyright.

The data, depictions, events, descriptions, and all other information forthwith are considered to be true, fair and accurate unless the work is expressly described as a work of fiction. Regardless of the nature of this work, the Publisher is exempt from any responsibility of actions taken by the reader in conjunction with this work. The Publisher acknowledges that the reader acts of their own accord and releases the author and Publisher of any responsibility for the observance of tips, advice, counsel, strategies and techniques that may be offered in this volume.

Table of Contents

Introduction 9

PART I - UNDERSTANDING HYDROPONICS 11

Chapter 1: What Is Hydroponic Gardening 12
- Gardening Without Soil 12
- When Hydroponic Gardening Is the Right Choice 13

Chapter 2: Hydroponics Throughout History 17

Chapter 3: The Science of Hydroponics 21
- The Photosynthesis Cycle 21
- The Needs of Plants 22
- Hydroponics and Growing Your Plants 23

Chapter 4: Hydroponics vs. Traditional Gardening
.... 24
- The Level of Control 24
- The Growth of Plants 25
- The Cost 26
- The Environment 27

Chapter 5: Introducing Hydroponic Builds 28
- Deep Water Culture (DWC) 28
- Wick 29
- Drip 31
- Ebb and Flow 32
- Nutrient Film Technique (NFT) 34

PART II - STARTING YOUR HYDROPONICS SETUP
.... 37

Chapter 6: Everything You Will Need to Build a Hydroponic Garden 38
- Growing Tray 38

Reservoir *39*
Air Pump *41*
Air Stone *41*
Growing Medium *41*
Monitoring Equipment *44*
Nutrient Solution and Fertilizer *46*
Lighting *46*
Timer *47*
Water Pump *48*

Chapter 7: Choosing Your Hydroponic Garden 49

Considering Space *49*
Considering Resources *50*
Considering Cost *50*
Considering Expandability *51*
Considering Reusability *51*

Chapter 8: DIY Builds on a Tight Budget 53

Building a Budget-Friendly Deep Water Culture *53*
Building a Budget-Friendly Wick Garden *57*
Building a Budget-Friendly Glass Jar Kratky Garden *59*

Chapter 9: Other Common DIY Builds 62

The Drip Garden *62*
The NFT Garden *66*

Chapter 10: Buying Your Own Hydroponic Garden 70

How Much Space Do You Have? *70*
What Kind of Garden Do You Want? *71*
What Are You Growing? *71*
How Much Are You Willing to Spend? *71*

Chapter 11: Maintaining Your System 73

Daily Maintenance *73*
Weekly Maintenance *74*
Monthly Deep Clean *75*

Chapter 12: Avoiding Beginner's Mistakes: Tips and Tricks for Your Hydroponic Garden 77

Not Paying Attention to Water Parameters 77
Ignoring the Differences for Each Plant 78
Entering the Room during Dark Periods 78
Skipping the Regular Maintenance Checks 79
Not Lighting Properly 80
Ignoring Sanitary Practices 80

PART III - PLANTING YOUR HYDROPONIC GARDEN 82

Chapter 13: Nourishing Your Plants: The Key to Perfect Produce 83

EC 83
pH 84
Macronutrients 84
Micronutrients 86
Selecting Your Fertilizer 86

Chapter 14: Choosing the Right Light 89

Common Lighting Requirements 89
Compact Fluorescent Lamps (CFL) 90
High Intensity Discharge (HID) 91
Light-Emitting Diode (LED) 91

Chapter 15: Preventing Pests 93

Spider Mites 93
Aphids 94
Thrips 94
Fungus Gnats 95
Whiteflies 95
Fighting the Pests 95
Preventing Infestation 96

Chapter 16: Troubleshooting 98

My Plant Has Rusty Leaves 98
The Leaves Are Turning Yellow 98
The Leaves Have White Spots 99

The Leaf Tips Are Burning *99*
The Leaves Are Wilted *99*
The Leaves Are Curled *100*
Plants Are Growing too Tall *100*
The Leaves Turn Purple After Flowering *101*
The Flowers Are Rotting *101*
My Plant Isn't Growing *101*
The Roots Are Brown *102*

Chapter 17: Starting Your Garden: Last Minute Skills You Need to Know 103

Germinating Your Plants *103*
Cloning Your Plants *105*
Pollinating Your Plants *106*

Chapter 18: Best Hydroponic Herbs for Beginners 108

Oregano *108*
Basil *109*
Parsley *109*
Cilantro *110*
Green Onion *110*
Chives *111*
Dill *111*
Fennel *112*
Sage *112*

Chapter 19: Best Hydroponic Fruits for Beginners 114

Strawberries *114*
Blueberries *115*
Tomatoes *115*
Watermelon *116*
Bell Peppers *117*
Cantaloupe *117*

Chapter 20: Best Hydroponic Vegetables for Beginners 119

Lettuce *119*

Spinach..*120*
Beans *121*
Broccoli *121*
Cauliflower..*122*
Kale *122*
Bok Choy *123*
Onions *123*
Carrots *124*

Conclusion... 125

BONUS

To get the

"15 Indoor Gardening Secrets"

Guide for Free,

use this link and you will receive it immediately:

https://bit.ly/15IndoorGardeningSecrets

Enjoy the Reading!

Introduction

Do you want to grow your own plants? Have you been worried in the past that the plants that you would like to grow are not going to tolerate the area that you currently live? Do you feel like you do not have the right space or the right climate or the right amount of time that you would need to ensure that your plants thrived?

If so, think again. There are options for you. All you truly need to give to your plant is enough water, enough light, and enough nutrients to thrive. Anything else can be tweaked if you know what you are doing. If you live in the wrong climate, all you have to do is grow indoors, where you can use climate control to maintain the right kinds of temperature. Do you live somewhere where the soil is not very good for growing, or perhaps the land is not flat enough to garden? That's fine too—you do not need vast plots of land to ensure that you can grow your garden into something that is productive, nor do you have to live in areas that will have the perfect climate. With hydroponic gardening, you can grow indoors in a controlled environment, meaning that you will no longer have to worry about the very climate that you are exposed to. There are alternatives that will allow you to grow indoors at any scale. Your only limit is the space that you have within your home.

This book is here to introduce you to the topics of hydroponic gardening. It will teach you all of the basics that you will need to know to get started. You will learn about what hydroponic gardening is, how to get started with hydroponic gardening, and the best traditional gardening techniques that you can take advantage of in order to ensure that your plants will thrive in just about any climate. From understanding what hydroponic gardening is to being able to build your own garden and everything that you will have to do in order to make sure that your plants will thrive, this book will help you.

All you have to do is commit to getting started, and you, too, will be able to master the art of hydroponic gardening for yourself once and for all.

PART I

UNDERSTANDING HYDROPONICS

Thanks for choosing this Book, let's start the Journey!

Make sure to leave a review on Amazon if you like it, I would really love to hear your thoughts!

Chapter 1: What Is Hydroponic Gardening

Hydroponic gardening is one of the best ways to get your plants to grow, whether you have the option to grow in soil or not. Hydroponic gardening itself is highly effective—it is great at producing larger crops than ever before. It allows you to better grow your crops and allows for your crops to grow quicker than ever, all because you eliminate half of the processes that your plants will need to go through.

When it comes down to it, hydroponic gardening is highly, highly effective in a wide range of scenarios, and because it is so highly effective, you can also usually get the crops that you will want, no matter where you live. Within this chapter, we are going to take a look at what hydroponic gardening is as well as why you should make the choice to try out this kind of gardening yourself.

Gardening Without Soil

Hydroponics is the art of gardening without soil. It takes the fact that plants require nutrients from the soil and provides those nutrients through the use of water. Water that is filled up with nutrients is provided to the plants directly at the roots in all sorts of different methods—it can work in several different ways, but at the end of the day, they all work with the same principle—they all work to allow for gardening to occur without the need of any soil because the roots get everything that they need.

Removing the soil can be a great way to allow for correcting all sorts of problems that you are likely to face. You will be able to reduce the rate at which your garden contracts disease because you will not be having it spread through the soil. Your plants will not have to waste valuable time and resources in trying to maintain root structures that are spread out enough to allow them to receive the nutrients that they will require. Rather, they will be able to grow far more conveniently in other ways instead—they will be able to ensure that they do properly get to meet those nutritional requirements all in one simple way—they do so by absorbing from the nutrient solution itself.

Aside from just removing disease, removing the soil will also enable you to eliminate a wide range of pests and weeds as well. You will not provide an environment that is very conducive to allowing either of these situations occurs, and because of that, you eliminate that from being a problem.

Essentially, removing soil from the situation entirely can actually make your life much simpler than it actually is; you can ensure that you are able to spend less time worrying about many of the problems that you would otherwise face in a traditional soil garden. You do not have to try to fertilize the ground based on gut feelings; you know what the nutritional values of your nutrient solution are instead. You do not have to worry about whether your plants will get hit with some sort of freeze or other debilitating occurrences—you will know that they will be safe and sound indoors with you in an environment that you will be able to control completely and that affords you all sorts of flexibility that you will need to ensure that your garden will thrive.

When Hydroponic Gardening Is the Right Choice

Hydroponic gardening is the right choice in a wide range of situations that can greatly benefit anyone. Firstly, if you have the space for a wide-scale garden outdoors, you may want to consider making use of a hydroponic garden in the first place just due to the fact that they are so much more successful than the other forms of gardening. Even if you have the space to build and grow outside, you may want to consider the fact that you will want to grow in a greenhouse with hydroponic methods just due to the fact that you will get better results. Nevertheless, if you are in any of these situations, you may want to consider that using a hydroponic garden is going to give you the best possible results.

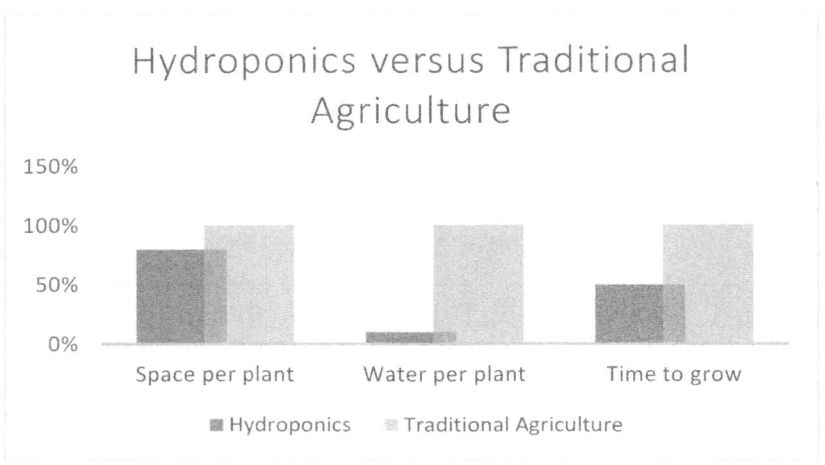

When you are short on space

Hydroponic gardening will limit the amount of space that you will need to grow your garden. Because of the way that they grow, the plants do not require the use of any sort of extra effort on your part. They do not require you to have massive levels of soil built up to allow your plants to spread out. Instead, you can reduce the space that you will need significantly just by growing in a hydroponic setting instead. This means that you will be able to grow more in less space. Even better, there are many different methods that can also allow you to grow vertically as well. Methods such as the NFT method will allow for you to be able to build in ways that allow for stacking up of the system entirely, meaning that you can have several levels of the gardening growing in one place.

When you want to avoid wasting water

If you live somewhere that you know is short on water or in areas where freshwater can get expensive, using a hydroponic method is actually something that you can do to ensure that you are able to better garden. You will be able to ensure that your garden will develop in a way in which you are more prepared; you will know that your garden will be designed and able to grow in ways that will enable it to reserve water rather than wasting it. Essentially, the water that you will use will be highly recycled over and over again, with you only emptying out the water that you use after about a month. This means that your water will go further. Even better, because you contain the water to just one place, you know that you are not losing that water to other elements such as evaporation or anything else that would slowly eat away at the water that would have been used.

When you want higher crops

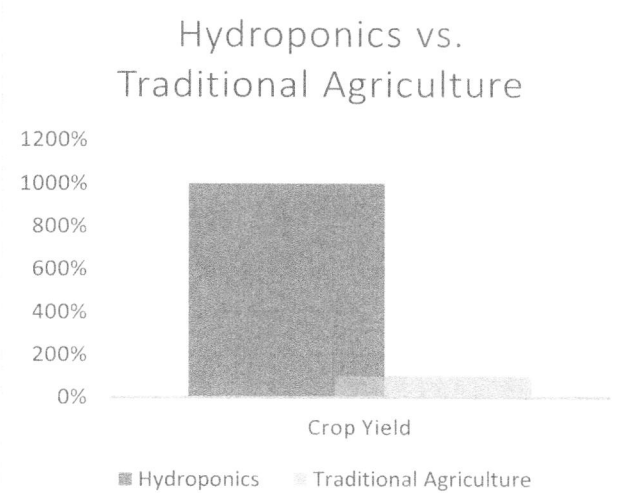

The crop yield for a hydroponic garden can be as high as 10x the amount that you would see in other situations. You can see that your plants will be able to grow quicker, use less space, and that translates into getting more out of the space that you have in the form of several different harvests within a smaller space, and even better, the yield for each individual crop is usually higher as well, leading to overall gains.

When you want to save time

While there is a lot of up-front startup cost and time that you must invest, and while you have weekly maintenance that you must do, as well as monthly attempts to sanitize everything that you need, you will find that your garden is going to save you time. You will not have to weed out your garden. You will not have to constantly water your garden several times per day. That will enable you to spend that time that you would have otherwise spent doing other things instead.

When you want to garden in a city or a setting in which you do not have a yard

You will be able to garden in just about any setting if you know what you are doing. You do not have to have land, or even a dedicated space to grow your garden. You simply have to have a small space that you will be able to leave your plants to grow. If you can guarantee that you have that for yourself, your plants will be able to thrive in just about any setting that you decide to put them in.

Chapter 2: Hydroponics Throughout History

Hydroponic gardening is nothing new to history. Even back in the days of the Aztecs, people were making use of hydroponic principles. The idea of growing plants submerged in water is something very common; people were able to make use of these principles far before the science of why it worked was ever known.

The ancient Aztecs, settled on Lake Tenochtitlan, were unable to grow traditional crops in such marshy land. They could ensure that they were able to grow crops their own way on the lake. Likely inspired by the growth of plants within lakes already, the ancient Aztecs set out to design a system in which they created rafts, consisting of both roots and reeds topped with the soil from the bottom of the lake. These rafts were just buoyant enough to float atop the lake, and the roots which held the rafts together were able to come right into contact with the water, which is filled up with the natural nutrients that are created through the nitrogen cycle. Essentially, the plants were fed a nutrient solution based on the waste of the fish in the lake. As a result, the crops would grow greatly atop them, allowing for the water to nourish them. This was the perfect option for them—they were able to make use of the fact that they could not grow in the soil and they discovered that they could also tap into the natural cycles of the earth, ensuring that the food that they were going to develop would be enough to provide them with what they needed.

There are reports that in the late 13th century, China had similar gardens developed—they were making use of floating gardens to grow their own vegetables to allow for them to grow on lakes or other areas that were too wet to develop. This was documented heavily by Marco Polo, writing that he had discovered this as he traveled through China on his own. This allowed him to acknowledge that there were methods of gardening that were different.

However, the first mentioning of hydroponic gardening is as far back as 600 B.C with the mentions of the Hanging Gardens of Babylon. Built in Babylonia, as the name implies, there were gardens that were built along the Euphrates River. The land in this particular region was far too dry to tolerate for proper plants, especially due to the fact that rainfall was highly uncommon. However, people, with necessity becoming the requirement for ingenuity, were able to figure out a way in which they could properly allow themselves to garden. They created a massive system designed around chains and pulleys that allowed for them to pull buckets of water up to the top of a massive structure and then pour it downward, allowing for all of the water to trickle downwards, allowing for all of the plants to get the water that they will need. This is like a modified drip system, allowing them to better be able to provide for all of their plants, giving them what they needed.

In more modern times, however, the philosopher and scientist, Sir Francis Bacon, discovered that soilless gardening was actually something that was viable. It showed that he was looking into these methods of gardening without soil, and the time that he took to do so went into also looking at other systems as well. Other people made it a point to research as well. John Woodward, an English scientist, discovered in 1699 that plants grown in all sorts of different water solutions usually had all sorts of different results. The water taken from rain, the water from the river, and the water that had been mixed with soil all grew plants at different rates. The plants that were grown in water mixed with soil allowed for the development of healthier plants. They were able to grow better because of the nutrients that were provided to them from the soil. The soil being mixed into the water caused there to be higher levels of minerals inside of them.

However, it was not until a Berkeley scientist by the name of William Gericke began to focus on hydroponic systems that it really came into modern limelight. He discovered that he could provide nutrients to the plants that he was growing with the use of a water solution and, in doing so, created massive tomato plants. He initially came up with the term aquaculture for this—however that name had already been reserved by the people that were farming aquatic organisms. Instead, he came up with hydroponics from the roots for water and the roots for labor or working.

In 1938, this research was expanded further, and it even led to the development of commercial uses of hydroponic gardening. There were several plants that were grown in mineralized water on Wake Island—this was an island used commonly for refueling at the time, but the land itself was not fit to allow for the development or growth of anything nutritious. There was no soil on the island at all, and as a result, they could not garden. Shipping food regularly to these people who lived there to manage the island was not always cheap, nor was it highly recommended as a way to process everything, and as a direct result, they were able to come up with other options instead. They were able to grow these plants in large tanks of mineralized water instead, allowing for hydroponically growing food for those that lived there.

This same sort of usage became commonplace—several other islands in the Pacific Islands began making use of these methods to farm when troops were stationed throughout them during World War II. It allowed for people to be fed and kept in areas that they otherwise would be unable to be within.

Nowadays, however, there is no doubt about it. Hydroponic gardening is one of the most efficient methods of gardening that exist. It is sustainable since it does not damage the land the way that traditional gardening does. It does not cause problems for people or cost inordinate amounts of money that cannot be maintained. It simply exists there for people to make use of.

When you garden in these manners, you know that you are able to take complete advantage of these many different benefits that exist. You are essentially able to better deal with what is going on. You are able to better grow with the parameters that you are in, and as these experiences have shown, you will even be able to better grow these plants in areas that otherwise would be unable to sustain them. This means that this could be a viable option to bring agriculture to deserts in which gardening is difficult. It is a viable option in areas that require other sorts of backups. It is possible that these methods are something that you can take advantage of; you can learn to really control the way in which you are able to garden, and you are able to bring gardening to all sorts of places that would otherwise struggle.

Even commercially today, hydroponic systems are highly common. You can see that many of the plants that you would buy and many of the herbs that are grown year-round in greenhouses are grown in hydroponic methods that allow for the plants to better develop. Because of the convenience, the speed, and the turnaround, as well as the long-term savings that are there when you are not constantly wasting your water, this is a great alternative to traditional growing methods. You can continue to turn around product all winter. If you want to grow a field of strawberries in your basement in the middle of January and have freshly picked berries, you can do that. All you have to do is make sure that you know what you are doing to ensure that everything stays alive.

Chapter 3: The Science of Hydroponics

Hydroponics works because of the way that plants themselves work. You must be prepared to understand what it is that you are truly doing when it comes down to having a hydroponic garden. When you grow your own hydroponic setup, you know that you are creating a situation in which you are better able to control everything that your plants need. Nothing is left to nature when you grow in a hydroponic setting; you are able to control it all artificially. You control the light that your plants get. You control the nutrients that they require. You control the way in which they grow and the way in which they thrive. You are able to recognize that ultimately, the way that you do grow your plants is crucially important.

The Photosynthesis Cycle

The plants that you grow work on the photosynthesis process. This process allows the plant to essentially create their own chemical energy. People and other animals require sustenance—we must consume something else to break it down to get energy. However, plants use a process known as photosynthesis to take the light energy that they get from the sun and convert it into a chemical form that will allow them to develop the sugars that they require to grow. This process is most commonly described with the following equation:

$$6CO_2 + 6H_2O \longrightarrow C_6H_{12}O_6 + 6O_2$$

This process allows for the plant to take light energy, along with six molecules of carbon dioxide (CO_2) and 6 water molecules (H_2O) to create one sugar molecule ($C_6H_{12}O_6$) and six oxygen molecules (O_2). This allows for the development of the sugar that is going to be used for the plant to thrive. This will essentially allow for your plants to sustain themselves, so long as they have that ready access to water, carbon dioxide, and light.

Of course, that sugar is not going to help them if they do not also have the other nutrients that are required to help grow all of the various parts of their bodies. If they do not get those extra minerals as well, they will not be able to develop.

The Needs of Plants

With hydroponics in mind, then your plants require access to several different components if they want to be able to grow properly. You will need to be able to provide these three components if you want your plants to be able to develop, and without them, your plants will struggle. At a bare minimum, your plants will require you to provide them with water, air, and nutrients that will help them to grow and thrive.

The water is easy—you can get that in many different places and is nothing that comes as any sort of surprise to anyone involved. The water allows for the photosynthesis process to be completed and also allows for the plant to develop properly.

The air is also easy—it is incredibly difficult to actually properly deprive a plant of access to the air. The plants will take in the air around them through their leaves, breathing in the carbon dioxide that is produced by other living things and then using that CO_2 to produce the sugars that it needs during photosynthesis. The plants then breathe out O_2 as their waste—the form of oxygen that we as people require to breathe.

However, there is one more important element here as well that you must be able to consider—you must not forget to include the fact that the plants that you will be growing will require nutrients. They cannot create themselves and their cells out of nothing, and that is where the nutrients that they require come into play the nutrients allow them to develop themselves. This is traditionally drawn in through the soil and into the plants by the use of the roots. However, it does not have to come from the soil directly. So long as the plants have access to nutrients somehow, they are able to thrive. This means that you must be able to give that access in one form or another. Some people will aerosolize nutrient solution into the air, in a form known as aeroponics. Some people will grow their plants in nutrient-rich soil. Others still make use of the nutrient solutions that we will be discussing in depth within this book. It does not matter how the nutrient solution is developed, so long as it is.

Hydroponics and Growing Your Plants

When it comes to hydroponics then, scientifically, there is no reason that you have to provide soil in any form. While it has been used as a fertilizer for the water, mixing soil into the water to see how well the plants would grow in that condition, it is not a requirement. You can grow your plants in all sorts of ways that will better help them. You can allow for your plants to develop in many different ways, meaning that you will be able to better process them for any situation.

Hydroponics is just one way that you can grow plants, but scientifically, it is highly effective. It is very good at ensuring that the plants that are growing are able to develop properly and thoroughly. You will be able to grow your garden in all sorts of different manners—all that truly matters is that you are able to find the right method that works for you. If you can do that, you know that you will grow a successful, fruitful (sometimes even literally!) garden.

Chapter 4: Hydroponics vs. Traditional Gardening

When it comes right down to it, there are many different reasons that you should choose hydroponics over traditional soil gardening. Hydroponic systems work without soil, but that also means that they are able to develop far quicker than you would normally see a plant grow. You are able to grow your plants significantly quicker and you are able to be able to make highly fruitful gardens, but at the same time, there are startup costs that are there. We are going to go over several ways in which the two of these forms of gardening clash from each other so you can begin to make your own informed decision about what it is that you will truly want to do with your own plants. Do you want to grow a hydroponic garden or is traditional soil-based going to be right for you? Sometimes, soil-based plants are able to be grown matter for those that are growing. They are able to better work for some people, especially if you do not want to put in a massive amount of money or if you are only growing for a small project. Even then, however, there are hydroponic methods that will require very little startup and very little cost if you really want to get started with them. All that really matters is that you will be able to choose what is right for you at the end of the day.

The Level of Control

The level of control that you are able to get with each form of gardening is different. If you are looking for a more traditional approach or you are interested in the experience of not knowing what will happen as you garden, going with a method that will work for soil may be right for you. You may love the idea of all of the work that will go into this form of gardening, and that is entirely up to you. The best part about this all is that when it comes to gardening, you are able to choose any methods that you want. You are able to recognize that you can ultimately have complete and utter control over the experience. You can have the control to decide that you want it to be somewhat random and dependent upon how nature decides to work with you. You can also decide that you want an environment in which you are able to control everything around you. It is up to you to determine which of these that you would prefer. You are able to decide if what really matters to you is being able to develop that level of control, that means that you can dictate each and every aspect of the gardening experience.

When it comes to hydroponics, you get utter control. You can control the lighting and the weather. You are able to control the day and night cycles as opposed to being at the mercy of the sun and the earth's rotation. You can determine how many nutrients that your plants have access to if you wanted them. You can determine just how much or how little you want to grow. All of this is entirely within your control, and if you are a perfectionist that loves the idea of taking complete and utter control of everything that you are doing, this is perfect for you. If you do not like that idea, however, you will likely find that you would prefer other methods instead.

The Growth of Plants

Between both traditional and hydroponic methods of gardening, there is almost no contest—hydroponic plants are usually able to grow quicker than their soil-based peers thanks to the fact that they get everything that they need to be provided right to their root rather than being required to process them other ways. Essentially, the roots do not have to grow out as widely as you would otherwise be required to grow. You do not have to worry about the way in which your plants are going to develop or if they are getting enough nutrients because you know that at the end of the day, they are. They have everything given to them, meaning that they can redirect their energy to the leaves themselves rather than to the root system.

The vast majority of plants will develop better in the hydroponic setting—this is just a fact. However, you can find some plants that do better in soil. Some root vegetables, like potatoes, tend to be much better suited to being grown in soil. While they can be grown hydroponically, they typically develop into much smaller plants than they otherwise would if they were grown in other methods instead.

The Cost

The cost of how the startup will look actually does put hydroponic gardening at a major disadvantage. The startup costs of a hydroponic garden, especially if you are attempting to create a wide scale development, is oftentimes quite high. This is thanks to the fact that growing a garden is not exactly cheap. You will need to buy up many different supplies that will cost you money to get, and you will also have to put them together into a system that is going to be functional. This can be pricy, both in time and in money. However, this is not something that is typically a problem if you will be growing more than one harvest. You will be able to make up the startup costs that will go into a hydroponic system just in the productivity of the garden itself. A large-scale garden is likely to produce a massive amount of produce that you can harvest, meaning that you will be getting a return on it.

Over time as well, you must also look at the costs associated with lighting, the fertilizers, the water, and any pesticides that you may choose to use. If you are going to be making use of any of these, you may decide that it is not actually worth it to garden in certain ways. However, you may also determine that the garden is one that you are happy to maintain. You will need to weigh just how much money you have to dedicate and just how many plants you are looking at growing.

Again, there are gardens that you can develop at any price point—you will be able to develop gardens in smaller scales that will not actually cost very much. You can set up systems in your windowsill that will allow for the process to occur without having to actually spend the money on lighting. There are options out there if you are worried about breaking your budget, but if you want a large-scale garden and you do not have the money for the resources, you may be better off with the lesser yield of the traditional garden. That will be something that you will have to determine for yourself.

The Environment

Finally, the environment is another major difference between both hydroponic and traditional gardening. Typically, hydroponic gardens are indoors. You can grow them outdoors, but most people prefer them in either a greenhouse or in a setting that they are able to control, such as a room or a basement in their home.

This is significant for one major reason—if you are gardening in your home, you can usually recognize that your garden is going to be better controlled. You are able to grow your plants in any environment and during any season, so long as you are able to make sure that you keep your system aligned with what it is supposed to look like and the temperatures that your plants will need.

In a traditional garden, you are limited by your environment. You must first have the land that you will need to grow. You will not be able to really grow a full traditional garden if you live in a city or if you are limited by other features such as climate. However, you can eliminate that with your hydroponic garden. You will truly be able to garden just about anywhere that you go, meaning that you can better develop your plants and ensure that they are able to grow better than ever.

Chapter 5: Introducing Hydroponic Builds

There are many different hydroponic builds that you can make use of. Ultimately, what matters the most is that you choose one that will not only meet your needs, but also ensure that you are better able to grow within your space constraints. You will be able to ensure that you can grow in just about any environment if you are able to make use of these methods—all that matters is that you are able to better control the system and ensure that it is one that is going to work for you.

Within this chapter, we are going to address the five most common hydroponic builds for beginners. These methods are the most common ones that you will find being used, and they will ensure that ultimately, you can grow in just about any environment. The five methods that you will discover in this chapter are the deep water culture, the wick, the drip, the ebb and flow, and the nutrient film technique. Each and everyone have their own purposes and some are easier to build than others. Do not worry—even if your budget is tight, there are options that will work for you. You just have to ensure that you are able to recognize that you are choosing the right ones for you.

Deep Water Culture (DWC)

The most common beginner's method of growing a plant hydroponically is the use of deep water culture. This is essentially created by simply submerging your plants' roots right into a nutrient solution that they will remain submerged in. the idea with this method is that the roots will be underwater the entire time that they grow. This can create some serious challenges, however—when you grow in this method, you must be able to recognize that you need to keep your plants underwater, but you must also recognize that your plants still require oxygenation to some degree. Without this method working for you, you will not be able to ensure that your plants will thrive.

The key to this method is the fact that you must include an air pump and an air stone. Without them, your roots will essentially drown. Submerged too long and deprived of oxygen, your roots will eventually rot and die, unable to keep themselves alive. You will then run into this problem each and every time that you are engaging in your plants being exposed in the water without properly aerating them. If you do not aerate them enough, you will find that they will not be able to develop.

This means, however, that this method of gardening is also tied entirely to the use of electricity. If you do not have access to electricity regularly for any reason or you are in an area that does not have constant steady access to electricity, this can be a major problem. Your plants are not meant to tolerate long periods of being submerged most of the time, and if they are, they are going to struggle to develop and grow.

Keep in mind that plants that grow in this method are somewhat limited. You will need to be providing yourself with very specific plants to make use of this sort of method. Most of the time, this is really only suited to herbs or green leafy plants that are harvested well before flowering. This is just due to the preferences of the plants-- not many flowering ones actually do well with complete and total submersion.

Wick

The wick method is an entirely passive method. This method allows you to essentially create a system in which you are able to grow your plants without having to do much of anything other than keeping your reservoir, the part of the system that holds the water, filled up with the nutrient solution that it will require. Essentially, you will put your plants into a growing tray that will hold them all. The growing tray will be full of an absorbent growing medium—an inert substance that will allow for your plants to develop and thrive. It essentially supports the roots of your plants, allowing them to continue to grow with ease. You will then have a wick of an absorbent material going between the growing tray and the reservoir, the area in which you are storing all of your nutrient solution for future use. Essentially, you will put them together, allowing for this development to work properly.

The idea with the wick method is that the nutrient solution gets wicked up to the top of the system. The nutrient solution is pulled all the way up and into the growing medium, which will then naturally absorb the solution and allow your plants to thrive. The roots will essentially work to absorb all of the solution from around them, and that will provide them with the nutrients that they will require.

The catch with this method is that it can be difficult to do on a large scale. It is entirely electricity-free, meaning that you do not have any parts that will require you to keep them running, with the exception being if you are using grow lights. However, the entire system will allow for your plants to better develop if you can ensure that the wicks that you have chosen to use are going to be sufficient enough to allow for the movement of enough liquid. Because you will have to manually thread in the wicks for all of the plants that you grow, if you are growing a wider scale garden, this may not be the right method for you. It may not be something that is going to work well if, for example, you wanted to make a larger garden. You may also not want to use this if the plants that you are growing have a higher need for water than others. You want to ensure that you will have enough water for the plants that you have, and that will require many wicks for plants that are highly water-dependent. You must weigh your pros and cons and determine if you really want to use this method for a plant that will require more than the wicks can really feasibly provide.

Drip

The drip method is perhaps the most popular method for people that are growing larger levels of plants, especially in a commercial setting. Essentially, this is something that would allow you to slowly feed water to the plants that you are going throughout the day, or in some cases, constantly. This is important to keep in mind—if you want to ensure that you are constantly giving small levels of water to your plants that will not lead to them drowning in the water that they have available, this is a great option for you. However, you will have to do some fine-tuning to ensure that, ultimately, you will be able to grow what you are trying to get to grow. You need to tow that line between too much water, which can saturate your system, or not enough water, which can lead to other problems as well. You need to find that sort of middle-ground setting that will ensure that your system is going to work well for you.

The system is designed to have a small line of hose that is near each and every single plant that is set up in that growing tray. Next to each line of hose, there should some way for the water to pour out and slowly drip into the growing medium that your plant is planted within. This then allows for your system to better process itself. You will be able to ensure that your system is more secure. You will be able to ensure that your system will function better. You will be able to ensure that your system is likely to develop effectively in many different settings.

When it comes down to it, then this system can be quite useful. It is also a bit more intensive to set up if you do not know what you are doing. If you are a beginner, you may not actually be able to make use of this system effectively, especially if you are a bit more unfamiliar with the efforts that you would have to put into being able to control the way in which you garden. You want to be able to ensure that ultimately, your plants will get what they need and that you are not going to have any leaks.

These systems also make use of small hoses, which sometimes can get clogged up. Nutrient solution can sometimes create clogs of mineral solution that will essentially keep them from being able to flow from place to place within the system, which can be a major problem if you are not careful. However, in keeping this in mind, you can usually work around it. You will need to make sure that you take the time to check all tubing on a regular basis because the fact that these systems rarely make use of larger amounts of water within the growing trays at any given time also leads to the implication that your plants are going to struggle to thrive. You are going to see problems if your lines get clogged, even on a shorter scale, just due to the fact that they will dry up the plants quickly if you do not correct the problem. Plants are not meant to tolerate long periods of time in truly dry growing conditions, and if your system dries out too much, you can have some major problems.

Ebb and Flow

The ebb and flow technique is a great one that many people love to take advantage of as well. Like the drip method, it is a bit more difficult to run if you do not know what you are doing.

However, the hoses that are used are typically a bit larger with these, and they do not clog up as much. These systems work quite simply: They involve the use of a pump that will send water straight into the growing tray. The growing tray is filled up with medium that is not particularly absorbent—if it is too absorbent, you can run into problems in which the roots end up drowning or rotting because of the amount of water.

This system will quickly fill up the growing tray with nutrient solution, and then that solution will be allowed to drain back out over time, draining right back to the reservoir for future use again in the next round. Essentially, then, this has to be timed just right to be effective. If you want to make sure that you are able to better grow your system, you will need to figure out just how much water needs to be pumped and then you will have to ensure that you can set the timer to allow for exactly this amount.

The problems with this system arise when there are problems in setting everything up. If you do not program your system right, you can run into a situation in which you do not have enough nutrient solution going into the plants, meaning that the roots are not getting enough either. This is a huge problem—if the plants are deprived of what they need, they are not likely to grow very well at all. On the other hand, if you flow water into your system too quickly, you can run into other problems instead. You can accidentally flood the entire system, and while it is called the ebb and flow method, and it is sometimes called the flood system, you are not meant to literally flood the system. You do not want to be losing precious nutrient solution outside of your system or you will have problems. You want to ensure that your system is getting enough solution and is able to grow properly but is not flooding itself and wasting that solution. This sort of balancing act can be difficult to manage the right way if you do not know what you are doing.

Further, this system is just as dependent as a timer as some of the other methods that we have looked at, but that dependency also turns into a requirement for electricity that will mean that you cannot possibly get your system to grow properly if you do not manage to fill it up right. If your timer fails, you will have problems with the nutrient solution. You will either see the timer fail and allow for all of the liquid to flow out of the system and effectively flood some of it outside of the system entirely, or you can run into a situation in which the timer does not go off at all, creating another major problem if your plants do not get their recommended amount of water.

Nutrient Film Technique (NFT)

The nutrient film technique is another method that is highly popular in many situations, as well. It is commonly used by people that try to get a longer system in which they can grow a straight line on the same nutrient solution. Essentially, you will have a long tube of some sort, commonly made out of PVC piping, that is used to allow for the development of everything. You will be tasked with setting it up so that liquid will be allowed to flow down, thanks to gravity. This is a slight incline—only about an inch every several feet or so. However, that is enough for you to be able to create systems that are tiered if you know what you are doing. You can create a system that spirals around itself, creating a sort of helix shape in place, allowing for the plants to be grown one on top of the other. This is common with herbs in particular—it makes use of plants that do not grow very large at all and allows for them to be developed thoroughly.

In these systems, the nutrient solution is always being pumped up and out at a slow enough pace that there is only a thin line of nutrient solution left on the bottom of the tubing for the roots. The roots are then able to dip themselves into the solution to get exactly the solution that they want. This also leaves ample space for the roots to be able to get all of the air that they will need to keep themselves growing. Also, thanks to the fact that you will be able to keep your water flowing, you are constantly aerating it as well, meaning that there is less of a concern for the roots to drown.

Essentially, the biggest concern with this is ensuring that your pump will be strong enough to take the solution up through the top, flow throughout the entire system, and then allow it down through the system and back into the reservoir. The hardest part is ensuring that you can get the water high enough to reach the top of your system in the first place, and this will be the way that your system is limited the most. If you cannot get the system to work properly, you will have trouble keeping up with the flow, and that is a huge problem. You must be able to see the way in which your system will be able to keep itself running if you hope to succeed and that means that you must invest in the right pumping.

You will also be limited by electricity in this situation as well—without it, your system will not be able to thrive or grow. You are also limited by the fact that some plants are not very well suited to this method of growing. IN particular, plants that will require higher levels of support or trellising may become too heavy for an NFT method, especially because of the fact that the NFT is higher up than many of the others just to take advantage of the power of gravity to keep everything flowing. You will also be limited by the way in which your system will work. If you decide to grow plants that have highly stretched out roots, you can run into other problems that are going to hold you back. You must ensure that you are able to grow your plants in a way that will not create clogs, and plants that create winding root systems that are too large can really just clog up the entire system, blocking water and creating a backup that could potentially cause flooding in your system. You will have to be mindful of this.

This is also perhaps the most technical of the methods that we are looking at within this book and is not the greatest for beginners, especially if you are not already familiar with building equipment. You could build it if you wanted to, but if you are not interested in building a system yourself, this is probably not the one for you unless you were to buy one or buy a kit that was already designed for you.

PART II

STARTING YOUR HYDROPONICS SETUP

Now we are about to go deeper into Hydroponics Techniques

Chapter 6: Everything You Will Need to Build a Hydroponic Garden

When it comes to running your hydroponic garden, you will need tools and supplies. You will need certain materials to ensure that your system will be able to grow effectively, and if you do not have them, your system is not likely to work well for yourself. You must be able to ensure that you will have everything that you need on hand, and you may even want to have a second set just in case you will need a backup as well. This is imperative—if you really want to ensure that your system will grow properly, you will need to ensure that you will be able to trust that you have the equipment for it. Within this chapter, we are going to take a look at the most important equipment that you will need to have on hand to ensure that you can build the system yourself. While not all of these pieces will be featured in each and every one of the systems these are the most common pieces of equipment that you will need. Keep that in mind and make your list for everything that you will need to buy once you actually know what it is that you are doing and how you are going to do it in the first place. It is only then that you will be able to guarantee that you have everything all lined up and accounted for.

Growing Tray

The growing tray is the most basic piece of equipment that you will use. Thankfully, it does not have to be anything expensive either. You will be able to make use of anything that will support the plants that you are growing for your growing tray. Some people will use Styrofoam suspended above their systems. Other people make use of buckets, plant containers, or even bottles to create their growing trays and all things considered; there is no one right or wrong answer here on how you can do this. You do not have to worry about spending the big bucks on getting one unless you want to—you can choose to do so, but it is entirely optional.

The only consideration that you should remember when you want to choose out your growing tray is that it must be safe for food products. This means that if you are using plastic, you want to ensure that it is food grade. If you are making use of a system that is going to be built upon steel or some other sort of material, you simply want to ensure that it is something that you will be able to trust is not going to endanger the plants that you are growing. You want to ensure that your plants will grow healthily and will not be impacted.

You should also keep in mind that whatever you use should be safe to use in water. You do not want your growing tray to rust or to react with any of the nutrients that you are providing your plants—that could be a major problem for you. Instead, you should ensure that you know what you are getting will be safe in your hydroponic system. You can build one, or you can buy one. Some people, when they need larger-scale systems, will make use of food-grade intermediate bulk containers (IBC) to grow their own plants. They are able to cut the tote in half and use one half for the growing tray and the other half for their reservoir.

Reservoir

The reservoir is another important piece of equipment that you will need to ensure that your system will thrive. Thankfully, like the growing tray, this is another piece of equipment that will not have to break the bank. Your reservoir can be just about anything that will hold onto water, so long as you ensure that the system itself is able to be closed and is light-proof. You do not want light to get into your reservoir that is holding your solution. If you get light into the reservoir, you are likely to begin to develop algae, which can be a huge problem for you. While algae itself is not necessarily harmful, it can have harmful effects on everything. It will essentially be lowering the amount of available nutrients that your plants will not be able to access themselves. This is a huge problem—when you do this, you will run into a situation in which your plants will not be getting the right levels of nutrients, and they will fail.

Commonly, these systems are built out of just food-grade buckets on smaller scales, or on a larger scale; a tank meant to hold water or even a storage bucket from the store will serve well. If you have the perfect piece already at home but do not think that it will resist lighting, you can fix that problem as well—all you have to do is make sure that your system is guarded against the light. You will effectively just use spray paint to seal the entire thing to make sure that you have enough protection from the light.

When you choose out your reservoir, you must ensure that you pick out one that will be the right size, and the way to do that is actually quite simple. You want a container that will hold enough solution for all of your plants. At a bare minimum, then, you want a system that will be able to hold:

- ½ gallon per small plant that you are growing (small herbs)
- 1 ½ gallon per medium plant that you are growing (strawberry sized)
- At least 2 ½ gallons per larger plants, with more being necessary for the largest plants or the most demanding plants.

When you are choosing your system out, you will need to figure out how much space you have available and then figure out just how much solution you will actually need. Those numbers right there are a bare minimum as well. Many other sources may recommend that you double it, and many people with more experience commonly do double it up to ensure that everything is getting enough water to really thrive in their systems.

Air Pump

The air pump is a crucial tool for your deep water culture systems, and some people prefer to simply always aerate their nutrient solution, no matter what. You will essentially want to find any pump that is meant to provide the right kind of aeration for any aquariums that are of a similar size to your own reservoir. You do not have to buy an air pump that is specific to hydroponics, either—you can make use of systems that are designed to use in an aquarium, and you should get enough aeration for your own system. You will want to do that—if you cannot find one that is big enough or strong enough, you can simply add a second one as well to the system to ensure that your system is going to run properly. This is not difficult—just find one that will fit your reservoir.

Air Stone

Likewise, the air stone, which may or may not come with the air pump (make sure you check the box before buying to determine if you need one or not), is crucial. This is the part of the pump that will allow for the distribution of all of the oxygen throughout the system. If you can ensure that you are properly getting that nutrient solution aerated through the air stone, you will know that you are getting the proper aeration that will work for you. Again, there is not much to do here—just find one that works for you and fits into your space.

Growing Medium

The growing medium is highly dependent upon your own preferences. It is meant to be something that is inert so that it does not interfere with the gardening process. There are many different options, ranging from free if you were to gather some river rocks, all the way to quite pricy if you want some heat-treated clay or other forms of media that are highly processed to get to the point that they are at. You can choose these based on what it is that you are looking to achieve—you simply need to figure out which you prefer for your system and for the plants. Keep in mind that not all systems will require the use of a growing medium, and if yours does not, that is just fine. Now, let's go over the most common examples and choices that you will have for yourself:

- **Perlite:** This is highly common—it is usually added into soil itself to create aeration. It is a form of volcanic glass that is then heated rapidly to high temperatures. This then pops out bubbles, which makes it porous and quite light, allowing for the addition of air to the system. It is great for use in a wick system that will naturally absorb the solution while still allow for the development of the plants. It is also still able to provide the right kind of aeration that the plants will need as well. However, it is very lightweight and can actually begin to be blown away or washed away if you need to use a lot of water at all. It is commonly used as an additive to other media instead.

- **Coco coir:** This is a form of media that makes use of the husks from the coconut shell that would previously be deemed a waste that did not serve any purposes. However, nowadays, those husks get processed into what is known as coco coir. This is commonly formed into a dense sort of shaving that creates a peat-like consistency. If you care about organic materials, this is the growing medium for you. It is inert and does not break down much at all, making it highly efficient, and it is also able to retain air as well. When it does start to wear out, you can simply compost it, making disposal a breeze. However, this medium is highly absorbent and does not drain out well, so you will need to add perlite or vermiculite or something else that is highly aerating to it.

- **Vermiculite:** This is another form of mineral that is then highly heated up and treated into small pellets of aerated, expanded material that is great to use in a hydroponic setting. This is a great option for you—it is lightweight and holds water well. It does not, however, keep the same aeration that perlite does, and because of that, many people combine perlite and vermiculite together in a 50/50 ratio.

- **Rockwool:** This is commonly used for people that are interested in starting their own plants. The rockwool itself is highly effective at being used to ensure that the people are able to develop their plants from seedlings, providing the right amount of support and also ensuring that it does not absorb too much water. Even better, once you treat it to balance out the pH, it is highly nonreactive in the water that you have it in. Rockwool is created by taking granite or limestone and superheating it to its melting point. Then, that melted rock is taken and spun, much like cotton candy, creating the wool. It is then taken and pushed into bricks that can be used by gardeners. This is perhaps one of the most versatile of the methods that you can find.

- **Expanded clay pellets:** This is sometimes labeled HYDROTON or LECA (lightweight expanded clay aggregate). They are little pellets of clay that are taken and heated to make it pop, much like how popcorn would. This creates several small balls of a lightweight clay that will also be absorbent. They are lightweight but still heavy enough to avoid being floated away by the flow of your system. They also allow  for the proper development of the support system for the roots to ensure that the plants do not fall. These are also highly reusable. While expensive, they can be recycled and reused through sterilization, making them highly desirable.

There are, of course, other methods and materials out there as well. If none of these catch your fancy, there is a good chance that you will be able to find a different one that does.

Monitoring Equipment

In hydroponics, there are a few key measurements that you will need to take regularly. You will need to be able to check on the pH of your nutrient solution. You will need to keep track of your system's electrical conductivity. You will also need to ensure that you are able to take care of the system's temperature as well. This means that you will need several tools to help you with these processes. You will need to ensure that you are getting these systems built in place and guaranteeing that you will have the right equipment for the job. Without the ability to monitor, you will not be able to perfect the growing conditions that you are looking for.

- **Thermometer:** This is the easiest of the measuring equipment that you will need. You will want an aquatic thermometer to allow you to keep track of the temperature of your nutrient solution in your reservoir to ensure that it is kept right on track. You will also need a thermometer for the air in your growing area to ensure that you are not accidentally superheating your plants or causing them any other problems.

- **EC meter:** This is a piece of equipment that is designed to allow you to be able to record the electrical conductivity (EC) of the water. It is essentially measuring out the ions that are mixed into the water, which will then tell you the concentration of the nutrient solution that you are using. We will be going over this more later in the book.

- **pH test:** You can get this in many different forms. The pH of your system can also give you good hints about the concentration levels of your system. If you have too high or too low of a pH, you are going to see problems for your system. Your plants will have very specific parameters for the pH, and you will need to adhere to them the best that you can. You will want to check if your pH is either too high or too low every time that you do a check on your system as well as after adding fresh solution. You can get tests that will be a strip of paper that you dip into the solution, and it will be color-coded. You can also get tubes of water and mix drops of chemicals into them that will change the color to tell you the pH as well. However, there are also pens that you can dip in and digitally record what the pH is and that will give you the most accurate number.

Nutrient Solution and Fertilizer

You will also need to consider the nutrient solution of your system. This is a solution for the water that you are using for your hydroponic garden and the nutrients that they need, as the name implies. The nutrients are typically added in through the use of fertilizers that will then be fed to the plants through the roots. This is one of the most integral pieces of the entire system, and if you do not get the nutrient solution just right, your system will fail. Thankfully, we will be dedicating plenty of time to this concept later on in this book to determine how you can ensure that your plants will be getting the right nutrient solution that they need and getting the right kind of fertilizer.

Lighting

Lighting is another highly required part of this whole system. Lighting is also one place in your garden that you will want to avoid skimping on, if at all possible. You want to ensure that you are able to provide your system with everything that it will need, and that requires that you give it the right kind of lighting. If your lighting is wrong, your plant will suffer. If you choose a light that is not strong enough, your plants will not have enough energy that they will be able to convert from the light into their chemical energy in the process of photosynthesis—they will simply not get the nutrition or the energy that they will need to grow and function, which can be a major problem.

On the other hand, too much light can also scald the plants or cause them to bolt—this means that some plants may flower too early and in the case of many root vegetables and leafy greens, this can actually ruin the plants entirely, changing the taste of them into something entirely unpalatable. Because of this, you must be able to get the lighting right, and more people are likely to give their systems the wrong kind of light or not enough light than the right kind at all, and that is a huge problem. If you want to ensure that your system is going to grow into what it is meant to grow into, you must ensure that the lighting needs are met.

If there is a place for you to splurge, it is almost definitely here. You will want to get the nicest lighting that you can for your plants. While your plants are not really impacted by the type of container that you put them in or the kind of reservoir that their solution is kept, they do care about the lighting. The wrong light can destroy your garden before you even had a chance to really get started with it. This should always be your number-one priority in terms of quality and expense. There are several different types of lighting that you can make use of in the grand scheme of things, but we will be addressing this in a later chapter.

Timer

The timer is the part of your system that works almost like the brain. It will activate and tell everything when to turn on and when to shut everything down. You will be able to choose the timer that you want largely based on what you are looking for. If you do not mind going in every day to turn on or off the lights, that is fine, and you will not need much in terms of a timer. If you have a system that will require several times around the clock for it to turn on, however, such as the ebb and flow method, and you want to also allow for that automation of your lighting as well, you are going to want to make sure that your timer has enough plugs and enough settings for everything.

Ultimately, a timer is a timer, so long as it will turn on when it needs to and turn off when it needs to. All that matters here is that you get a reputable timer that you can trust, and you ensure that it is going to work for you.

Water Pump

Finally, you must also consider the water pump. For many systems, this is essentially the lifeblood of the entire operation. If you do not have a good pump, your system is going to fail, especially if you need to move water around. While not all systems require a pump, you still need to consider that some of them do, and if you do not keep that consideration in mind, you can run into other problems as well. You must ensure that the pump that you choose will have the pumping power that you will need to ensure that water will get where it needs to.

There are primarily two choices for you when it comes to pumps—you can get one that is submerged into the water or one that is outside of the system and has hoses attaching the reservoir to the growing tray. Ultimately, the one that you choose is up to you. However, most of the time, in a hobby or a beginner garden, you will be better off making use of the submersible pump instead. This will allow for water to cool the pump, and it is also typically a bit cheaper. It will get the job done. However, if you need more power or you are in a commercial setting, you may want to start looking at the external pumps instead.

Chapter 7: Choosing Your Hydroponic Garden

When it comes down to choosing your hydroponic garden, you have all sorts of options out there for you that you can make. It can be difficult to determine which kind of garden you want to grow for yourself, but thankfully, there are guides that can really help you to determine which kind of garden you want. If you want a garden that is larger or smaller, you can make that call. We are going to go over several considerations that can really help you to make the decision on which kind of hydroponic garden you really want at the end of the day. You will want to consider each and every one of the aspects that will be provided to you shortly so you can begin to determine which actually matters the most to you. This will enable you to figure out precisely what it is that you really want and what your space and budget can accommodate.

Considering Space

Space is perhaps the biggest limiter that you will have in any good hydroponic garden. Some of these methods, such as the DWC or the Wick are not very space-demanding. You could build either of them and leave them on a windowsill or on a countertop, and they would be fine to grow, for example, an herb garden. However, if you want more or you want a larger system, you are going to want to look at just how much space you want.

The NFT, for example, is highly effective for long and narrow spaces, especially if you also make use of the fact that you can use it on several levels so long as you have a pump that is strong enough. You may consider a large ebb and flow method if you have a big chunk of space all lined up.
Before you begin any build, however, make sure that you write down the measurements that you have available and do not go

over them. Make sure that you always ensure that your system will fit within the space that is available.

Considering Resources

You should also consider the resources or supplies that each of these systems will need. Some will be more draining on power, for example, while others are more or less designed to be set down and forgotten about. Consider the impact that any of these gardens are likely to have on your power bill. Something like the NFT that is constantly running a pump and lighting, for example, may be more expensive, or even out of your budget, than the DWC.

You should also consider just how many supplies are needed. Do you have a pump? Do you want to buy one? What about the tubing? Do you want something that only has a few pieces to assemble it, or are you happy with putting together something that is larger and more demanding? This is also important to remember and keep in mind—if you do not keep this in mind, you could have a problem.

You should also consider your time a resource as well—do you want a system that can be left alone for long periods of time, or do you want one that is perfectly fine being kept for a while? No matter the system that you prefer, you will want to make sure that you do not choose one that will require too much time on your part.

Considering Cost

Cost is another huge factor to consider as well. Just how much money do you have available to you? Some systems are incredibly simple to do on less than even just $10, or you may even have all of the supplies already for some of the easiest and cheapest DIY methods. However, some of these systems are quite expensive and demanding on resources. If you do not want to buy the entirety of the framing that you will need for an NFT, you may not want to be using it. If you do not mind the cost, then it may be fine.

Keep in mind that there are options at any budget. You simply have to be willing to accept them at the end of the day. Make sure that you know what your budget is and then stick to it, even if it is tempting to go over it.

Considering Expandability

Consider as well just how much you want your system to scale. A wick system could be great for you if you are just getting started, but if you are looking for a system that will grow with you as you continue to learn and as you decide to expand, it may not be right for you. The same goes for a DWC. While you can do these particular methods of gardening on a wider scale, they are not likely to be very effective or make good use of your time. You could, however, look at an NFT and see something that can be endlessly expanded, so long as you constantly provide enough nutrient solution for the entire system.

Essentially, you must consider how likely you are to continue to grow with your garden. If this is something that you are not going to expand upon, then some of the more stringent, smaller methods may be just fine. However, if you hope to turn this into something bigger as you get more practice, you will want to look at drip methods, NFTS, and even the ebb and flow as all of those are highly expandable and usable, even at commercial levels.

Considering Reusability

Finally, you must also consider just how much reusability that you want. How likely are you to reuse the garden after the first or second use? With some of the more expensive and time-consuming methods, you may find that it is not actually worth the money if you are really only going to use them once. If you are going to grow several harvests or make your hydroponic garden a staple in your home long-term, then an NFT or other more intensive and expensive methods may be just fine. However, if this is just an experiment with kids or designed for homework or a single lesson or occurrence, you may want to stick to some of the smaller, cheaper DIY methods that you are going to be introduced to shortly. There are some great options, but ultimately, you do not want to be spending too much money or attempting to keep yourself limited too much. Weigh the likelihood of how often you will continue to reuse your system before you decide on which to invest in.

Chapter 8: DIY Builds on a Tight Budget

Thankfully, DIY hydroponic gardening does not have to be expensive. On the contrary, there are many cheap builds that you can make with supplies that you probably already have all around your home. The three builds that you are about to be introduced to are the ultimate builds that can be set down and left to run themselves. While the deep water culture will require you to make use of an air pump, therefore requiring electricity, the other two options are electricity-free, so long as you do not have to rely on intense lights for the plants, and oftentimes, with small builds like these, you would be just fine leaving them in the windowsill to get some sunlight that way. As you read through this chapter, you can expect to be provided with a list of the supplies that you will need, as well as a guide to the steps that must be completed to create the build itself.

Building a Budget-Friendly Deep Water Culture

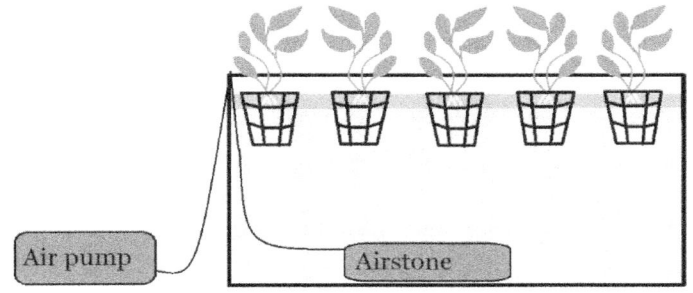

The first budget-friendly build that we are going to look at is the deep water culture. This is one of the easiest ways that you can get started quickly and easily—if you can mix your nutrient solution, assemble an air pump, and put some plants into the system, you can use this sort of garden with ease! This is a great starting point for beginners because it is so non-technical—you are simply leaving your plants in net pots, submerged in the garden.

This system will require:

- An opaque tote storage container and lid (commonly found in 18-gallon sizes at any big-box retailer, but any size will work here if it meets the water requirements for your system)

- An air pump and air stone

- Net pots (verify that these are the right size for the full plants that you are going to be growing)

- Growing medium of choice (a common choice is using expanded clay pellets on the bottom of the net pots, with cubes of rockwool for starters for seedlings placed atop the clay)

- Nutrient solution

- Tools to cut holes in the lid of the storage container

This build is quite simple. Keep in mind that, when assembling this, it is assumed that you already have plants ready. If you do not, you would simply assemble the system and wait to fill it with the nutrient solution until your plant starts, which will be discussed in Chapter 17: Starting Your Garden.

To build this setup, follow these steps:

1. **Gather everything that you will need:** It is always best to have everything all lined up and ready to go prior to starting. Make sure that your container that you will be using to create your reservoir is lightproof, and if it is not, you can treat it with certain light-blocking spray paints on the exterior to try to prevent light from penetrating to the nutrient solution. Also

ensure that you have all of the tubing that you will need for your pump, and the right size of net pots.

2. **Prepare the Growing Tray:** In this system, your growing tray is more of a big tray that will suspend the growing pots into the nutrient solution. Measure out the lips of the net pots that you are going to be using and cut just slightly smaller than them. You want the lip of the net pots to hold the pots up on the lid of the storage container, allowing the plants to be submerged without falling into the solution. Then, cut out the holes and ensure that they fit. Make sure that your pots are assembled at the proper space as dictated by the plants that you are growing.

3. **Drill a hole for your tubing:** Near the top of the container, you are going to want to drill a small hole, just large enough for the tubing for your air pump. This will allow for the lid to sit firmly on top of the container while still providing a way for your air pump to be looped through. This will be perfect for your system.

4. **Add the air stone:** At the bottom of the system, you want your air stone, or stones if you need more than one for your container to be placed. You will want each of these to work thoroughly to ensure that your water is well-mixed and aerated. Feed the tubing for the air pump through the hole you drilled and attach it to the stone with the other end attached to the pump.

5. **Prepare the nutrient solution:** This is one of the easier steps—all you have to do is follow the instructions for the nutrient solution of your choice. You will simply read the ratios that you will be trying to mix and follow the guidelines to make it happen. We will spend more time talking about the specifics to nutrient solutions in Chapter 13: Nourishing Your Plants. Make sure that you place your container where you want it to be, as once you add the solution, it will

be heavy and difficult to move. Add the nutrient solution to the container. You will want to fill it up enough so that it submerges the net pots without flooding when you do add the pots at a later step.

6. **Prepare the net pots:** You must now take the time to prepare your net pots. This is quite simple—all you will do is fill them up with your growing medium, preferably something that will not lose structure in water. Then, place your plants into the pots as well. The plants will be just fine if you leave them in the starting cubes of rockwool.

7. **Put it together:** Take the lid to your system and attach it to the reservoir filled up with the nutrient solution. Place each of your net pots into the holes that you have cut. Turn on the air pump.

8. **Allow the system to run:** All that is left is to let the system run. Use lighting if necessary, or leave in the sunlight if it is not. Make sure that you check water levels regularly, especially as your plants start to grow and begin to use up more water than they used to. Top up as necessary.

Building a Budget-Friendly Wick Garden

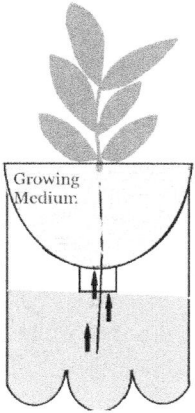

The wick garden is almost even simpler than the DWC just due to the fact that you do not need to do much cutting or setting up anything. It is as simple as adding your wick to the system and then allowing it to pull up the nutrient solution. Thanks to the passive nature of these systems, they are quite simple. While this particular build is going to make use of just an empty plastic bottle that you may have laying around your home, you can follow the same principle to build larger systems as well—you would just add more holes, more solution, and more wicks to the process. The most important part is that your growing tray is right above the reservoir so the wicks can pull up solution.

For this system, you will need:

- A plastic bottle (preferably 2-liter)

- A wick (Any fabric that will absorb liquid. Cotton ropes are common, but need to be replaced. Nylon is also common and will resist degradation and rotting)

- Nutrient solution

- Growing medium that will aid in absorption (vermiculite and perlite blend is the most common)

To build this, you will essentially be cutting the plastic bottle in half, nestling the top half with the bottleneck downward, and using the bottle as both the growing tray and the reservoir as well. It is quite simple.

To build this easy system, you will need to do the following:

1. **Cut the bottle in half:** To do this, you want to measure it out so that there is at least an eight-inch reservoir and then simply cut straight across it horizontally, as evenly as possible.

2. **Remove the bottle cap and prepare the wick:** You will then want to take the bottle cap and drill a hole straight into the center. This is going to be the entry point for the wick, connecting both the tray and the reservoir together. Your hole should be large enough that the wick will go through without fraying, but small enough that it will not simply slide right through it.

3. **Prepare the nutrient solution:** You then want to make sure that you prepare your nutrient solution and pour it into the reservoir of the system.

4. **Attach the lid and prepare the growing area:** Now, reattach the top of the bottle onto it tightly and make sure that the wick is secure. Invert the top and place it, lid side down, into the reservoir. Holding the wick upright, add in your growing medium. You want to make sure that you continue to hold onto it so that the wick does not fall and get stuck to the side or fall to the bottom. This will allow for optimum transference of nutrient solution.

5. **Add your plant:** All that's left is to plant your plant into the system. With this sized system, you are

probably looking at growing something small. It could work well for, for example, an herb plant.

6. **Optional protection from light:** It is highly recommended that you prevent your nutrient solution from being exposed to light just due to the fact that it can harbor algae. The best way that you can protect your little bottle garden is through making use of foil wrapped around it. This can be enough to lightproof your system to prevent the growth of algae

7. **Maintain water levels:** From there, all that is left is making sure that your water levels stay high enough to prevent the system from drying out.

Building a Budget-Friendly Glass Jar Kratky Garden

This next method is perhaps one of the simplest—you are simply growing right into a glass jar and letting your plant go and grow on its own. All you will have to do is the initial assembly, and the plant should do the rest of the hard work for you. This system is known as the Kratky method, and in this particular build, you will be assembling it in a simple glass jar. The jar could be repurposed from a pickle or condiment jar that you already have sitting around. You probably already have almost everything that you will need for this system already in your home.

To complete this build, you will need:

- Glass jars

- Nutrient solution

- Net pots

- Growing medium (expanded clay pebbles are usually recommended, or you can even just use some smooth gravel that will not fall through the net pots)

- Plants

- Something to cover up the jars (foil is easy and cheap)

This system is highly simple to assemble. It works best if you can make use of a net pot that is slightly larger than the lid of your system, as then you have no adjustments to make to the whole system come together. This is usually as simple as just measuring out the diameter of the jar's opening prior to choosing your net pots.

To put this together, you will want to do the following:

1. **Optional: Painting the jars:** If you want to paint your jars to prevent light from entering them, now is the time to do so. This then allows you to better prevent algae development, but if you do not want to paint them, you can simply cover them up with foil at the end

of the process, which will also allow you to take a look at the roots to ensure that they appear healthy.

2. **Filling the jars:** To begin, you will want to fill up your jars with nutrient solution. You should fill them almost to the top, leaving just enough space so that when you place your net pot within them, they will not suddenly flood or spill over. As always, follow the directions for the nutrient solution of your choice.

3. **Assemble your net pots:** You will want to now take your net pots and fill them up with your growing medium. Within the center of the growing medium, you will want to place your seedlings. If you do not have rockwool, you can simply insert your germinated seeds straight into your growing medium, provided that your medium will lap up the water, such as expanded clay pebbles. If not, you may want to consider the use of rockwool.

4. **Place the net pots into the jar:** This step is as simple as the name implies—just place the net pots right into the jar, ensuring that they fit firmly.

5. **Cover up the bottom of the jar, if not already done:** You want to block out as much light as possible!

Let it grow: Now, just leave the pot to grow. The Kratky method does not even require any additional water unless it runs out entirely—remember, it is meant to have definitive air and water zones.

Chapter 9: Other Common DIY Builds

While those first builds were perfect for someone just starting to dabble with the idea of growing their own garden, there are other builds that are usually a bit more technical. These builds usually work well on larger scales—you are able to grow far more in these just because of the way in which they do get set up. They are designed for those people who want their systems to be able to accommodate more, and these are also commonly involved in wider-scale agricultural growth as well. As you read through this chapter, you are going to be guided through the development of a drip, ebb and flow, and NFT garden.

The Drip Garden

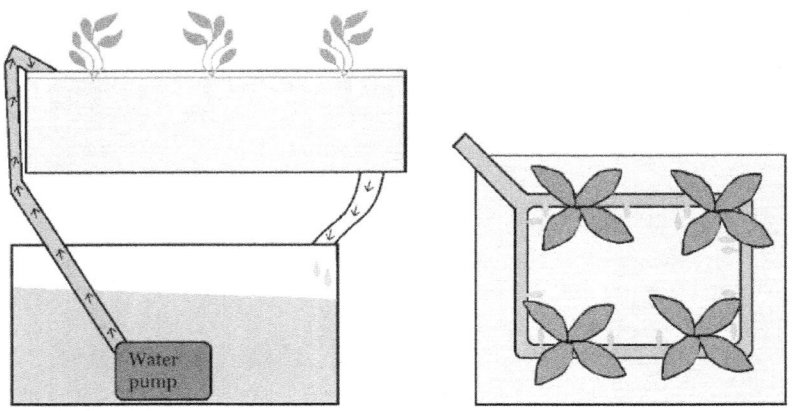

The drip garden is commonly used in hydroponic settings thanks to the fact that it provides the perfect amount of water to each plant, allowing them to get the water that they need without flooding, meaning that they get just the right amount of air as well. They can, however, be finicky due to the fact that the tubes can sometimes get clogged up. The guide that you are being provided here could also be adjusted to be an ebb and flow garden if you were to make a slight change to the timer—instead of having it drip feed, you would simply set it to run for longer to fill up the system and then drain back into the reservoir.

For this build, you will need:

- Grow tray of any size or shape to accommodate the plants that you intend to grow

- Reservoir large enough to provide water for the number and size of plants that you have chosen to grow

- Water pump: Submersible is just fine. Make sure to check the pump's ratings to ensure that it is powerful enough for the size of your garden and make sure it has a filter.

- Water filters—these are commonly just furnace filters or other mesh filters that are fine enough to keep the growing medium in place

- Air pump: you want to aerate the nutrient solution as well in the reservoir

- Tubing, grommet for the tubing, and splitters: You will want to ensure that you can split the tubing as much as you want with splitters that will fit the setup you have chosen.

- Growing medium (any—expanded clay pellets are a favorite, and it is highly recommended to have a layer of larger, easily drained growing medium, such as river rock, on the bottom underneath the pellets)

- Nutrient solution

- Timer to control the drip

All you will need to do once you have gotten everything gathered up is begin to assemble it all. This is not nearly as difficult as you may initially think, though it is more work than you would put into, say, a Kratky build just by virtue of all of the electronic parts that must be assembled and programmed.

To complete this build, you will need to do the following:

1. **Prepare the drainage line:** First, you will begin by assembling the tray and the reservoir. You need a hole on the bottom of one end of the grow tray. This is the drain. You will want to connect a line of tubing here with a grommet and secure the drain with a filter to prevent any unnecessary or unwanted draining of growing medium. The other end of the hose should then be attached to the lid of the reservoir through the same process of drilling a hole and attaching with a grommet.

2. **Prepare the grow tray:** Add a layer of a medium that will drain well, such as river rock, and then top the rock with the growing medium that you intend to use, such as expanded clay pebbles. Place your grow tray so that it is suspended above the reservoir and situate both the grow tray and the reservoir where you want them. Then, spacing your plants properly, add them to your grow tray.

3. **Prepare the reservoir:** Paint the reservoir if necessary, if it is transparent. Toward the top of the reservoir, you will need to drill two different holes—you need one on one side to allow for the tubing for the air pump, as well as the cord for the water pump. On the other side will be the hole for the tubing for the pump to deliver water to the growing tray. Measure the size of your tubing before drilling and keep the size the same, and set up a grommet for the tubing on this end.

4. **Prepare the tubing:** Take one long strip of tubing and attach it to the pump through the hole that you have created for it. Take this strip and bring it to the top of the growing tray. Split it here if you have two rows of plants, using a T attachment. You can also use a three- or four-way splitter if necessary as well. If you do not need a splitter, just extend the strip. You will then need to attach a strip of tubing for each row of plants that you are growing, extending the tubing, so it reaches around all plants. Then, using a fine-tipped screwdriver heated with a lighter's flame, melt small holes near where each plant will be in your growing tray. End the tubing with end caps that will prevent water from continuing to spray out.

5. **Prepare the nutrient solution:** Now, prepare the solution to the specifications of the system that you are using and add it to the reservoir, taking time to adjust the pH as required.

6. **Double-check:** Make sure that all of your wires and tubes are all connected where they are supposed to be and ready to go.

7. **Turn it on:** Turn on the air and water pumps, with the water pump connected to a timer. Set the timer accordingly based on the plants that you are growing.

The NFT Garden

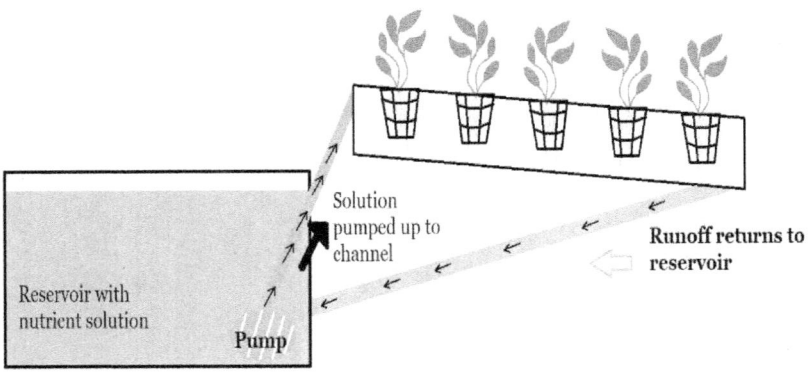

The NFT is, by far, the most complex of the methods that you are being guided through creating—but that is because to create an NFT garden, you must be able to build a frame for the growing trays—which in this case are actually PVC pipes or gutters kept at a slight incline to ensure that water is always flowing down them rather than anything else. These systems are highly effective and will provide the perfect mix of aeration and hydration, but they can take a bit of time to properly assemble. If you are already handy with the 2x4s and the hammers, this is probably just fine for you, but if not, you may want to skip this method or enlist the help of someone who is construction-savvy.

To complete this build, you will need:

- A plan detailing the shape and measurements of this build for the space that you have. This will vary greatly from person to person—just remember that no matter what, you will need a slight incline.

- 2x4 wood in the lengths that are required for the build that you have designed

- Sawhorse brackets
- Plant hooks to hold the piping
- 3-inch PVC piping to the requirements of your build—get enough elbows, straight pieces, and end caps for the design that you have created.
- Reservoir (70-gallon if possible, with a cover and painted to prevent light from entering)
- Water pump (submersible)
- Air pump
- Net pots (enough for all of the plants that you are growing)
- A drill
- Hole saw drill bit—just slightly smaller than the size of your net pots, so they do not fall

To begin, you will want to do the following:

1. **Assemble the frame:** This will involve you taking your plans and building the frame that will support them. The simplest ones involve creating sawhorse brackets, which will then have the tubes of PVC piping attached to them. You will want to build this to the specifications that you have designed that are going to maximize the use of the space that you have available to you.

2. **Preparing the tubing:** Begin by making sure that your pipes are at the lengths that are set out in the plan. Start by measuring out your straight pieces and cutting them, and then making sure that any elbows that you will be using are also the right size for the build that you are creating.

3. **Connecting the pipes and the tubing:** Then, you will want to begin attaching the pipes to the frame. This is commonly done with plant holders, but you could also make do with some brackets or any other method that you will want to use.

4. **Drilling:** When you have the system standing up, with the piping secured and attached to the frame, you can begin to drill the holes for your plants. Make sure that you leave ample space between the plants that you are growing to ensure that they all will have the necessary space to ensure that they will grow. Generally, you do not want your plants closer than 6 inches. There should be a hole in the beginning cap, where your pump will attach, and then you will need to drill a hole at the bottom of the end to create a drain back to your reservoir.

5. **Test:** Run some water throughout the entire system, pouring it into the beginning of the system, and watching to see if there are any obvious leaks. The piping should be secure, but if you notice a leak, patch it up with PVC cement.

6. **Set up the reservoir:** Now, it is time to attach the reservoir to the entire thing. You will want to ensure that your reservoir is underneath the system—it should be lower than the lowest point of the system, but also close enough to the entry point that your pump will be functional. Attach tubing from the ending of the pipes straight down to the reservoir. There should be no obvious kinking in the hose, and you want gravity to help ensure that the entirety of the solution drains back down. You will then want to attach the tubing from the pump to the top of the system.

7. **Fill with solution:** When you are confident that you have the system all in place, you can then begin to run the system. Fill up the reservoir with solution and turn

it on, looking for any signs of trouble. Adjust the strength of your pump until there is just a small trickle of solution flowing through the pipes.

8. **Add plants:** You can then add in the net pots, prepared with the growing medium of your choice and the plants that you are hoping to grow and place them in the holes.

Chapter 10: Buying Your Own Hydroponic Garden

Now, if none of the options that have been provided for you quite fit what you are looking for, or if you feel like you would rather not have to worry about building at all, you can also just buy a kit. These kits are designed to provide everything for you, so you are not concerned with how to make them work or what goes where. You will simply assemble according to the instructions without having to design your own system or worry about measurements. Sometimes, people find that simply buying a kit and having everything all provided in one nice, quick fell swoop is preferable just due to the fact that they do not want to be dealing with the way in which everything works—they just want to get started! When it comes down to it, there are a few considerations to make before you buy your garden that will help you find one that is exactly right for you, and this chapter is going to provide those benefits for you.

How Much Space Do You Have?

When it comes to buying a garden, the last thing you want to do is buy one that you then realize is not going to fit within the space that you have. You want to ensure that the garden that you have chosen is one that will fit, and because of that, the first step before buying your garden should always be to measure out the dimensions that you are hoping to fill. By making this your first step, you can simply double-check dimensions of all of the gardens that you are looking at, ensuring that you always cut out the ones that are outside of those parameters and ensuring that you are more likely to be successful than if you were to avoid doing so at all. This is perfect for you—if you want to ensure that you can properly manage your system, you will want to make sure it will fit.

What Kind of Garden Do You Want?

You should also think about whether any of the types of gardens that you have read about thus far actually appeal to you. Do you want one of these options? Do you want something that was not discussed? Do you want something that is meant to be a bit different? Do you want to look at other options, such as aquaponics or aeroponics? There are kits for all of those—you just have to keep your eyes open. Sometimes, buying a kit can make it easier to get started when it comes to making sure that your system is going to have more pieces. Some systems, such as the NFT, may also be easier to just buy thanks to the fact that you will not have to worry about measuring, cutting, and trying to get everything just right.

What Are You Growing?

Another key consideration when it comes to buying your garden is what you planned on growing in the first place. Some builds lend themselves better to certain plants than others. For example, NFT builds can be perfect for tomatoes, or drips can be perfect for strawberries. However, if you want to grow squash or something heavier, you may not want to go with an NFT—you would want something that would be easier to support. Think about what it is that you intend to garden before you start to purchase a system, so you do not end up with an elevated, PVC pipe NFT setup when you want to grow something that is too heavy.

How Much Are You Willing to Spend?

Finally, you must know what the ultimate price that you are willing to spend is. Hydroponic building kits, in which everything is all provided for you, can become quite pricy—sometimes even into the thousands of dollars, and you have to know what that sort of cutoff price is for you if you want to ensure that you are staying within the limits that you want for yourself. Also, try to make a list of any special features that you want to be included—some of these can even monitor all of the parameters that you would need to ensure that your system will grow properly.

Chapter 11: Maintaining Your System

When you finally have the system set up exactly how you want it to be, it is time to start looking at maintenance for the garden. One of the most appealing reasons to garden hydroponically for many people is the fact that it works well for anyone without too much upkeep. Really, on a daily basis, you will only need to dedicate a few moments to your garden to ensure that it is kept up with, and on a weekly basis, the maintenance done, so long as there is nothing noticeably wrong with your system, is minimal. The trick here is that you want to make sure that you are working in a way that will keep your system healthy and functional, so you do not have to stop, troubleshoot, and fix anything. Prevention is always the best process here. Within this chapter, you are going to be introduced to a daily, weekly, and monthly maintenance chore list. This is like your cheat sheet—it will tell you what must be done, when it must be done, and how often it must occur to keep your system functioning well.

Daily Maintenance

On a daily basis, you do not have much to do at all unless you find something is noticeably wrong. If everything looks okay when you do your daily walkthrough, there is nothing more for you to worry about. You will simply move on with your day, assured that your plants are growing well.

The daily maintenance list for your system includes the following tasks:

- Checking on all plants to ensure that they all look healthy and green. This is looking for any red flags that there is a serious problem with your system. If you do not see anything with a quick glance at your plant and it looks healthy, then it is probably fine.

- Checking the nutrient solution levels to ensure that nothing looks off. You will want to do this to make sure that you did not have a sudden, unexplained leak or any other problems that could be detrimental.

- Checking the pumps and hoses briefly. You will not need to do too much here—you just want to make sure that the pumps are on and that everything is flowing the way that it should.

- Checking the lighting and timers. Make sure that they are set to work properly as well.

Weekly Maintenance

Every week, you should do a more thorough check of your system. Weekly, you will be ensuring that everything is functioning the way that they are supposed to in order to be certain that your system will continue to work for you when and where you need it.

Every week, set aside a chunk of time to do the following:

- Checking all plants for signs of pests. You will want to take a closer look during this period of time to ensure that everything appears to be growing healthily and properly. You will be double-checking that there are no signs of pests during this check, and you should also take a look at the roots of your plants.

- Checking the water parameters. During this weekly maintenance time, you will want to test the pH, EC, and the water level. You will also want to take the time to determine whether or not your system has algae. You will do this by taking a look at the water and the tubing. Do you see anything that looks off?

- Adding more nutrient solution. On a weekly basis, you will also want to take the time to add in more nutrient solution to ensure that everything that you are growing is getting enough nutrient solution and that they will all have the proper nutrients that they will need. Remember that you should always adjust for pH after adding in the solution to get the EC back to where it should be for your garden.

- General cleaning. During this period, you should also be taking the time to do any necessary cleanup that you will need to ensure that your garden remains healthy and strong. Make sure that you are taking out all scraps of plants and double-checking that the floor stays clean as well.

Monthly Deep Clean

Monthly, you should choose one day in which you do a deep clean of your hydroponic garden. This is crucial—when it comes to being able to grow hydroponically, you want to ensure that your garden is going to thrive and that requires you to ensure that you are constantly growing your system effectively, and that requires sanitary measures. Generally speaking, hydroponic gardens thrive when they are kept sanitary. This is due to the fact that when you are growing with a hydroponic garden, you are trying to limit the potential for diseases to spread. You want to try to keep your system as clean as possible to ensure that you know that your system will be kept in good condition.

Monthly, then, you want to make sure that you take the time to stop, look at your garden, and then figure out how you can keep it clean and healthy. During this monthly clean, you will be flushing out the entire system to allow for a complete water change. By changing out the water, you know that your plants are getting the proper nutritional balance due to the fact that your plants will not drain all nutrients at the same rate. While you provide them with the right amount of nutrients, they all get absorbed differently, and that can lead to all sorts of discrepancies over time. Eventually, you will have higher levels of some nutrients than others, and that can be a big problem. The best way to keep it all balanced is with a complete flush of the system, which also gives you time to ensure that your system will be able to remain sanitized as well.

To complete this monthly deep clean, you will want to follow these steps:

1. Empty out the system and properly dispose of your nutrient solution

2. Take out all of your plants and scrub everything that you can get your hands on. Make use of brushes and sponges on handles to get areas that you cannot easily reach and sanitize the inside of your system.

3. Fill the reservoir up with a sanitizing bleach, dictated by the instructions on the bottle based on the gallons that you are filling up. Run the system for 30 minutes to an hour to allow for the sanitizer to flow throughout all of the tubing several times to properly disinfect.

4. Drain the cleaning solution and fill with fresh water to allow for a rinse. Run the system for another 30 minutes to an hour before draining.

5. Do an optional second rinse if you choose to do so. If not, add the plants back to the system and fill it up with fresh nutrient solution.

Chapter 12: Avoiding Beginner's Mistakes: Tips and Tricks for Your Hydroponic Garden

All too often, beginners fall for the same mistakes, over and over again. They tell themselves that these mistakes are not really as serious as they are made out to be. They tell themselves that there is no reason at all that they should be attempting to do follow the guidelines that they are given, or they try to make all sorts of exceptions that they assume will be harmless… But they aren't. Within this chapter, we are going to go over some of the most common beginner's mistakes that you are likely to encounter. You will see the example of the mistake that is made, and then you will be told how not to make that mistake in the first place, helping you avoid many avoidable problems. While we will all make mistakes sometimes, why make your mistake one that is easily avoidable?

Not Paying Attention to Water Parameters

The most common mistake people make is that they do not pay attention to the water parameters that they have in their nutrient solution. They may not pay attention to the temperature, which is highly important to ensure that the plants are able to get the proper oxygen uptake. They may not pay attention to the fact that their plants need very specific pH or EC and ignore them entirely, but that can cause all sorts of problems, too, and doing so can very easily kill your garden.

Remember that ultimately, your water parameters are what will determine the health of your garden. If you want to ensure that your garden is effective, you want to make it a point to ensure that your garden will be given the right kinds of parameters to keep it alive and keep it thriving. Remember, your plants will only produce harvests that reflect the quality of their growing conditions!

Ignoring the Differences for Each Plant

Some people also make the mistake of not paying attention to the fact that each and every individual plant that you are growing will have its own specific parameters. They will all have different needs in terms of temperature, lighting, and nutrient solution, and you will need to meet all three of these to create the optimum growing conditions for the plants to ensure that they will, in fact, grow properly. If you cannot do that, you will find that your plants will struggle to thrive and survive.

Make sure that you always know exactly what your plants will require. Make sure that when you are growing several plants within the same space, you ensure that they have very similar parameters that have enough overlap that you know they will survive and thrive together. If you are unsure about these parameters, don't worry—we will be taking a look at some of the best plants to grow and their parameters shortly!

Entering the Room during Dark Periods

Your gardens will frequently feature all sorts of dark periods in which they are able to take the time that they will need to grow uninterrupted. This will enable them to have the space that they need to grow and is directly related to the lighting requirements. Your plants rest when they are kept in the dark, and this is a crucial part of their growing cycle. This helps them to redirect energy to areas other than photosynthesis, such as growing properly. If you enter the room during a dark period, all you are doing is opening up the room and exposing the plants to light—no matter how little you think that you are adding in, it is still not in their best interest.
Instead, you must remember to only enter the garden when it is lit. This will prevent you from accidentally exposing them to light when they are supposed to be resting. While, in an emergency, going in to check would not necessarily kill the plants, it will cause problems if you regularly go in without

regard to your plants and their need for darkness sometimes. Try to respect this time as just as sacred as you would like your own sleeping time treated. You would not like being interrupted from your sleep either—so do not do it to your plants.

Skipping the Regular Maintenance Checks

Oftentimes, people decide that the maintenance checks can wait, or they are not important enough to follow through with. They may decide that their system has always been fine and assume that they will continue to be fine as well. However, the point of these regular maintenance checks is to ensure that your garden is able to thrive. The whole idea behind them is to make sure that if you do catch a problem, you catch it early on so you can prevent it from getting worse. It is far too easy for a hydroponic garden to fail, such as if the nutrient solution were to stop flowing for even just a day or two, drying out and suddenly depriving the plants of their nutrients and water long enough to potentially do irreversible damage. You need to be doing regular checks to prevent this from happening so you do know that your plants are taken care of—and yet, far too often, people fail to do so.

If you feel the urge to skip your maintenance check, do not do it. It is never worth the few minutes that you will save, especially if something goes wrong. Your maintenance checks are like insurance—they are there in case they are needed, and sometimes, you may never need them at all, which is perfectly fine, but you always want to be prepared in case you *do* need them. When you are prepared for that, you can usually ensure that your system will thrive, all because you were able to prevent them from dying. You will be able to step in at the first sign that something is going wrong. You will be able to prevent complete failure of your garden, and that is compelling.

Not Lighting Properly

Some people do not bother to invest in lighting. They assume that all light is created equally—but that is not true at all. Lighting is one of the most important parts of your entire system, and if you get it wrong, you risk serious problems.

Pay attention to Chapter 14, and invest in lighting. Make sure that lighting is given all of the consideration it deserves—which is enough to ensure that you get it right. Your lighting is crucial to your system.

Ignoring Sanitary Practices

Your system's success hinges upon you not introducing disease to it, and that means that you must ensure that you keep it sanitary. All interactions with your system should involve you firstly washing your hands, especially if you were just interacting with the outside world prior to entering your garden. However, some people do not think about this at all—they do not consider the ways in which plants require certain parameters to remain healthy or that you can introduce disease if you never sanitize your tools. Think about it—would you trust a doctor that never washed his hands or that used unsterile needles to give you vaccines?

Chances are, you would never return to that doctor. Just as doctors must remain sanitary for your health, it is your responsibility to remain healthy for your own plants as well. You must work hard to ensure that no matter what, you take the time to keep your own system healthy. Make sure you always wash your hands prior to handling your plants and always sanitize anything that you are using within your garden. If you are going to be collecting cuttings, for example, or trimming your plants, you must always sanitize your tools and make sure that they are cleaned when you move from plant to plant to prevent illness. You should also always quarantine the plants that you get from other places prior to introducing them to your system to avoid accidental infections. Allow your new plants to remain outside of the system for at least two weeks to ensure that they are not infected with anything at all.

PART III

PLANTING YOUR HYDROPONIC GARDEN

You're one step away from being a Hydroponic Gardening Expert

Chapter 13: Nourishing Your Plants: The Key to Perfect Produce

Now, you know how to choose your garden and how to build your garden. You know what goes into gardening and how to avoid making fatal beginner's mistakes. All that is left is to go through the details of growing your garden, and this chapter is here to walk you through some of the most crucial points in the entire practice. You are going to be looking at how to nourish your garden, looking firstly at EC and pH, and then moving on to understanding the nutrients that your plants will require. From there, you will learn to look for the right kind of fertilizer for your own garden to make sure that you choose the best ones that will work for you.

EC

Electrical conductivity in a hydroponic context shows how well your water will be able to conduct electricity throughout it. It helps you to understand the concentration of your solution so you will be able to get a better idea of how effective it will be. It measures the potential that electricity will have to be able to pass a current throughout water. Now, you may be thinking that water is meant to be a great conductor of electricity—and that is not entirely true. Water itself—pure water without anything else in it—is horrible at conducting electricity and will have a base measurement of 0.0 when you use an EC meter. However, when you start to add nutrients or minerals to the water, they ionize it; they add the potential for the electricity to be carried.

Essentially, the entire purpose of the EC of your system is to determine the concentration, and therefore what the nutrient levels are. The nutritional value that you add to your system is through the nutritional salts that you get as fertilizers and add to the system to ensure that the system can then support itself. Generally speaking, you can more or less generalize that 1.0

mS/cm, the common measurement for EC, is roughly 1 gram of salt to 1 liter of water.

pH

pH is another common measurement that you will have to deal with when you measure out your nutrient solution. It determines how much hydronium ion is present—water itself is a pH of 7.0. Less than 7 becomes acidic, and over 7 is said to be alkaline. This will help with the absorption of elements and therefore goes hand in hand with EC. The pH of your solution will determine whether the plants will be able to uptake it or not. If the pH is wrong, the plant will not be able to properly take in the nutrient solution, meaning that it will not grow properly. For most plants, the pH is likely to be somewhere between 5.5 and 6.5, and when those levels are not maintained, the primary nutrients that your plant will require will not be as available.

While your system's pH is likely to fluctuate, especially when you are actively adjusting the EC, it is important to note that you can manage the pH if it gets out of range. There are products known as pH Up and pH Down that can help you to shift the solution to the pH zone that it is supposed to be at. If you find that your nutrient solution is regularly at pH levels that are too high or low for the plants that you are growing, it is highly recommended that you adjust your system to get it back into that range, following the instructions included on the bottle.

Macronutrients

Your plant will have several nutrients that are deemed macronutrients. These nutrients are essential to your plant's survival, and they are required in higher levels than the micronutrients that you will be introduced to shortly. Typically, you can expect to see macronutrients divided into two categories: Primary and secondary.

Primary macronutrients NPK

The primary macronutrients are also sometimes referred to as NPK—Nitrogen, Phosphorus, and Potassium. These three nutrients are the ones that are commonly seen on the front of all fertilizers in the three-number ratio. The ratio stands for the percentage of each of these three nutrients, in order. This means that a fertilizer that says 10-12-14 would have 10% nitrogen content, 12% phosphorus content, and 14% potassium content. This is important to keep in mind, especially if you are trying to come up with the right way in which you can understand what your plants will need to thrive. Nitrogen is the most important element, and it allows for the growth of the plants themselves, as well as the creation of the chlorophyll that gives plants their characteristic green color. Phosphorus allows for the development of DNA to help with processing it as well as creating the DNA that goes into flowering. Potassium is commonly used to allow for the plant to process CO_2 uptake and allows for the activation of important enzymes for the plant to function.

Secondary macronutrients

Of course, there are also several nutrients deemed secondary as well. These are nutrients that are still absorbed in higher quantities, but a bit less than the primary three. The secondary nutrients are calcium, Sulfur, and magnesium, and all three of these have their own crucial important points as well. Calcium is required to ensure proper cell development. Sulfur creates proteins that will be used to help with enzymes and vitamin production. Magnesium is crucial for oxygen creation during photosynthesis. Potassium is necessary to help plants with their ability to photosynthesize as well, leading to protein synthesis.

Micronutrients

Beyond those macronutrients, there are several other micronutrients that serve very important roles as well, though they are required in lesser increments. You will need to ensure that your plants get all of the necessary micronutrients on top of everything else to really ensure that they are able to grow and thrive.
The most important of these micronutrients include:

- **Zinc:** This allows for the development of chlorophyll and enabling the plant to metabolize and process nitrogen

- **Boron:** This allows for the plant to, in tandem with calcium, create cell membranes, as well as helps with the reproduction process

- **Iron:** This allows for help with energy and nitrogen fixation, along with also being important with the creation of chlorophyll

- **Manganese:** This helps with the growth of the plant and aids in creating oxygen during the photosynthesis process.

Selecting Your Fertilizer

When it comes to selecting your fertilizer, you have two main options that you can take advantage of. You can make use of dry fertilizers—these are simply mixed into your water to create your nutrient solution—or you can make use of liquid fertilizers—which are concentrated liquid that is mixed into your water to create your nutrient solution. They each have their own pros and cons, and you will have to weigh them to determine which is right for you.

Dry fertilizer

Dry fertilizer is the cheaper of the two options, and it is perfectly acceptable to make use of. The trick here is that when you use a dry fertilizer, you are going to have to keep in mind that you will have to mix it thoroughly and you may have to measure out several different fertilizers at the same time when you go to use it. Typically, these fertilizers are found in separate counts, with differing amounts being required for each of them, and you will have to figure out which ones really matter the most for you. This can be great if you want to complete customizability. It is also the more space-efficient option between the two. You are only ever storing dry powder, which typically takes up far less space than a concentrated liquid.

Liquid fertilizer

Liquid fertilizer is oftentimes more convenient just because you usually just measure a liquid amount and dump it into the right amount of water. Because it is already liquefied, it is easy to emulsify into the water to create a nutrient solution, whereas it may take longer with a dried fertilizer, meaning that you will have no choice but to take your time with it. When you use a liquid fertilizer, you are going to pay a convenience fee—it is easier to use, but that also usually means that it is more expensive to buy as well. You will also have to keep in mind that you will have to store that liquid fertilizer somewhere as well, and it will take up more space, especially if you have larger gardens that will need larger amounts of fertilizer.

Choosing your own

When it comes to choosing your own fertilizer, you have to sort of weigh the pros and cons. Dry fertilizer is cheaper, but it is also a little more intensive to use—though not by much. You will have to measure out several salts, though it may sometimes be blended into one mixture. You will have to blend those salts until they saturate the water to create your nutrient solution as well, and that takes time and effort. However, it also takes up less space. Liquid fertilizer, on the other hand, costs more and takes more space, but it is simpler to use. They will both ultimately get the job done well enough, so you will simply need to figure out which you prefer personally to ensure that you get the right one for yourself. If you prefer to save money and do not care much about the effort that you will have to put in, then using a dry mixture is probably in your best interest. If you want it to be as foolproof as possible, buying liquid mixture may be your best bet.

Chapter 14: Choosing the Right Light

The lighting that you make use of in your own hydroponic setup is perhaps the most important decision that you have to make. Out of everything that could make or break your system, lighting is perhaps the easiest. Plants will grow if their nutrient solution is not quite right. They will still usually grow if you use the wrong kind of build for the varieties that you have chosen. They will even usually still grow if the temperatures are a bit off from what is required. However, one thing is true: If you get the lighting wrong, your plants will really struggle. They need to have the right kind of lighting if you want to be able to grow them, and the best determiner of the garden's success is usually getting the lighting just right for what you are growing. Within this chapter, you are going to be guided through the process of choosing out the right kinds of lighting for your system. You will be looking at the three most popular options that people use right now, as well as taking a look at what you can expect to be asked to provide within your own garden setup.

Common Lighting Requirements

When it comes to getting your lighting just right, there are two key considerations that will help you to determine what it is that your plants will need. These are the intensity and duration of the lighting.

Intensity

This refers to how bright the light is. You will need to get the intensity just right to ensure that your plants will grow effectively. Luckily, you have two ways in which you can readily adjust the intensity of your lights. You can control the wattage of the bulb in use, or you can make it a point to shift the space between your lighting and your plants. Adjusting for longer distances can lessen the intensity of the lighting while moving your light down closer to the plant can increase it. This is usually known through terms such as "full sun," "partial sun," and "shade" when you are looking at the guides for plants—that can determine the intensity of light that each of your plants requires.

Duration

This refers to how long your plant will require lighting. Typically, this is in relation to the season in which your plants grow. Usually, plants that grow in the summer will require longer periods of time in sunlight, while plants that grow in the spring or autumn, or even in the winter, are likely to require less time in the light. You can adjust accordingly through the use of a timer.

Compact Fluorescent Lamps (CFL)

CFL is one of the types of lighting that you can choose from when it comes to getting the lighting just right in your system. Typically, these are not commonly used these days, though they are energy-efficient, and they do last longer. These bulbs will produce light readily, but that light is not particularly strong. If you use a CFL, it is usually because you are looking for a cheap option that does not require any special equipment, but at the same time, cheap is rarely a good idea.

Larger plants typically struggle with CFL—they do not provide enough light to really get as deep into the plant as the other options that you have; you will need more of these lights if you really hope to make use of them, which may defeat the purpose if the problem was a matter of the equipment being available in the first place. If you must use one of these, try to aim for over 6500k to get the right spectrum, and even then, these bulbs are rarely suited for anything that is expected to flower.

High Intensity Discharge (HID)

HID lighting can be found in two different varieties depending upon the spectrum of light that you want. If you want redder lights, you will want to make use of high-pressure sodium varieties, or if you want to make use of a bluer end of the spectrum, such as if you are trying to grow vegetables, you will want the metal halide lighting instead.

Each of these forms of lighting is known as high intensity discharge. They are lights that involve bulbs filled up with gas, which, when heated, ignites. The ignition and the burning of the gas then creates high-powered, intense light. This light, of course, also produces high levels of heat and consumes high levels of energy as well. However, it is something that is highly effective at lighting your plants if you can get it just right. It will help you ensure that your plants get light that is closer to the sun's natural spectrum than the CFL will provide. You will also need to keep in mind that you will also need other equipment as well. You will need to be able to provide a ballast, which helps support the system by adding power to them without allowing for the power level to get too high.

These forms of light are great for any plants, but the fact that they will naturally create and emanate heat can be a major problem for many people that will need to also be mitigated in some way, shape, or form, and that can be difficult for some people. You will need to be mindful if you choose to make use of a HID.

Light-Emitting Diode (LED)

Finally, the last particular form of lighting that is used in hydroponics is actually the most modern, and consequentially, potentially the favorite at the moment. LED lighting is able to produce nearly an entire spectrum of light without increasing temperatures, making them highly effective, especially if you are making use of plants that require lower temperatures. Because LEDs will not heat the air around them and they are also very energy efficient, they have become very popular.

Of course, that popularity comes along with a cost. These are the most expensive option on the list—for good reason. They are highly efficient, not only with electricity and temperature, but also with the fact that they are typically able to last longer. They do not die nearly as easily as the other lighting options, and they are able to be used over and over again. If you are not afraid of having a bit of a price barrier to get over, these are a great option for any garden.

Chapter 15: Preventing Pests

Hydroponic gardens may be resistant to most common pests because they are indoors and, therefore, out of reach of many of them, but they are not entirely immune. There are several different pests that can, and commonly do, infect hydroponic gardens, and they can be difficult to keep up with or prevent. Some of these arise simply due to the fact that they do not have any natural predators in the system. Others are brought in accidentally with a new plant. Hydroponic gardens are no strangers to pests—after all, where there are plants, there are usually bugs as well. Within this chapter, we are going to take a look at five of the most common indoor pests that you are likely to find on your plants in your own hydroponic garden, and we will tackle what can be done to help mitigate disaster. Keep in mind that prevention is almost always easier than being able to eliminate the pests after they have infected your plants, and proper hygiene and sanitation is always the key to doing so.

Spider Mites

Spider mites are the most common pest that you are likely to encounter. Unfortunately, they can do massive amounts of damage to a plant, and they are capable of destroying leaves, 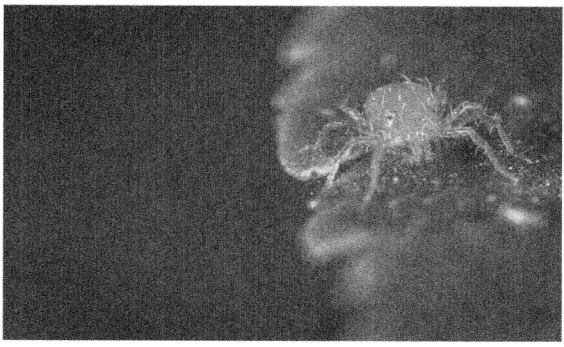 and potentially even the entire plant itself. Spider mites are tiny—they are less than a single millimeter long, and they are incredibly difficult to find if you are not paying close enough attention. They are little red arachnids that are so small that you will likely notice their signs of damage long before you see them. Typically, you will either see damage to the leaves or you will see webbing all over the tips of your plant, much like spider webbing, and that is your cue to investigate. They normally hide underneath the leaves of your plant, and one of the easiest ways to check is to wipe away at the underside of the leaves that you suspect are infected. If you see blood with a tissue as you wipe the plant, there is likely a spider mite infestation that will need to be taken care of somehow.

Aphids

Aphids come in several different colors—they are commonly green, but also occasionally appear in grey or black as well. Nevertheless, they still do damage to your plants when they are able to suck at the  plant's leaves. As they puncture the leaves and drink, they oftentimes leave behind little yellow splotches, and eventually, the whole leaf turns yellow and falls off in an attempt to defend against the damage.

Thrips

Thrips are a bit larger than spider mites, but not by much. However, they are also quite difficult to identify. You will want to look for signs of black spots atop your leaves. If this happens, along with the browning of leaves, you probably have thrips. They are pale and almost leaf-colored, skinny insects. They usually exist in groups, and that makes them so dangerous. They will all eat along the same plant and do serious damage. However, if you touch the plant, you will likely see them all fly off.

Fungus Gnats

Fungus gnats themselves are rarely dangerous, but their babies, the larval form of the gnats themselves, are typically quite damaging. They eat the roots that they have lain around, and that leads to all sorts of damage to the plants. When the roots become damaged, there is room for infection to spread throughout them. There is also room for the plant itself to die. While the gnats will stop eating when they mature, they will still lay their own eggs around the roots to provide food for their next generation.

Whiteflies

Whiteflies appear as tiny white moths that are actually somewhat easy to see. However, because they can fly away and spread throughout the entire room, they are quite difficult to keep track of. This can be a huge problem—if you are not careful, they can spread throughout all of your plants and do serious damage. You will be able to see this regularly—your plants will have white splotches on their leaves, and may even begin to yellow.

Fighting the Pests

Of course, just because you have identified a problem with pests in your garden does not mean that you have to throw in the towel. You do not have to give up on your garden, nor do you have to start all over. While you certainly can choose to discard a single plant or a handful of plants, if you notice that you are starting to harbor pests, there are a few other methods that you can try prior to this.

Spraying with water

Especially if you have noticed that your infestation is not particularly large yet, you can try spraying off the plants that you have, knocking off the mites or aphids, and removing them from your garden. They will simply fall off of the plant and have a hard time getting back to it. Of course, this is useless if the pest that you are trying to get rid of can fly.

Sticky traps

For flying pests, you can make use of sticky traps. These will allow you to trap the pests before they can reproduce further in your system. This may be a slow process of removal, however—and you may also want to consider adding sticky traps to the bases of your plants as well to stop pests before they can make the problems worse than they already are.

Pesticide sprays

Some people are highly against the addition of pesticide sprays to their own gardens, but they can be effective. You can also, however, try to make your own pesticide sprays. Some of the most common include the use of neem oil and eucalyptus oil. These will work to prevent pests from wanting to be in your area in the first place. They will be repelled from your garden, keeping it safe.

Adding predators to your system

You can also help your system by simply releasing good predators into it as well. For example, ladybugs are great at eating aphids and other pests, and by adding them, you can help your own garden by adding a natural element to it.

Preventing Infestation

To prevent the infestation at all, however, there are a few things that you can remember to do. Firstly, never take plants from outdoors. You should never try to use plants that you have found outside for your indoor garden, as this will often introduce elements into your garden that you were trying to avoid, such as those pests that you are trying to avoid. You can further help by ensuring that you keep your plants clean and healthy. By ensuring that they have everything that they will need to grow and thrive, you know that they are going to be more resistant to the pests in the first place, and the clean environment can help to prevent the infestation. You could also use pesticides or natural essential oils as a preventative as well, if you choose to do so. No matter the method that you choose, however, you want to make sure that you choose it because you want to use it.

Chapter 16: Troubleshooting

Sometimes, even the best, most meticulously maintained gardens will run into problems. This is only natural when you involve nature, after all. However, you can figure out what is going on with your garden relatively easily if you have a guide that you can use to figure it out. Within this chapter, we are going to go through some troubleshooting—it will be listing out common symptoms, and then discussing the most common causes so those problems can then be fixed without too much effort or too much frustration.

My Plant Has Rusty Leaves

Rusty spots are little brownish splotches across the green surfaces.
They have many different common causes, including:

- **Bugs or pests:** If bugs and pests eat at the plant, they will cause brownish spotting where the plant has begun to die

- **Deficiency:** This is usually due to a problem with either roots or nutrient solution. Check the roots first and then the solution. If the roots are brownish, you can usually assume that the nutrient solution needs to be balanced out.

The Leaves Are Turning Yellow

When the leaves turn yellow when they are not supposed to be, it is usually a sign of oxygen deprivation—especially if the yellowing is happening near the bottom of the plant. It is a sign that you will need to fix something with your water, or it could be that you have fungus covering up your roots and making it problematic for your plants to absorb what they need.

Check on the roots. If they look slimy, brown, or black, they are likely the problem, and that problem was most likely caused by mold or disease. If not, you will want to double-check your nutrient solution. There is a good chance that your plant is simply deficient in nutrients and you can fix the problem with just a little bit of effort.

The Leaves Have White Spots

White spots on leaves are almost always mildew, and they are bad. This is a sign that your plants are struggling to develop at all. If you see white dots, you are going to want to first check to see if you can see any signs of pests, and if not, then add some fungicide.

The Leaf Tips Are Burning

Sometimes, the tips of the leaves of a plant begin to burn, typically related to the nutrient solution. This is almost always a problem with the solution being too concentrated. It is oftentimes a sign that there is a salt buildup and that salt is hurting the plant. If not the nutrient solution or the roots, it could be that the light is too intense, especially if the leaves themselves look excessively burnt. You will want to check this as well. It could also be a sign that your nutrient solution is being drained too rapidly and that you require a larger reservoir to hold more water to prevent this problem with salt concentration.

The Leaves Are Wilted

Wilting leaves is oftentimes a sign that the plant is getting too hot or too much light. You will need to make the appropriate adjustments to ensure that you get the temperature right. Do not forget the temperature of the nutrient solution in your check.

The Leaves Are Curled

Curling leaves are rarely good things, but they can be quite telltale. Upwardly curved leaves are typically the end result of a problem with the pH. Remember, when pH is off, there is a deficiency in nutrients, typically because of the problem with the plant not being able to take in the nutrients when the pH is not right in the first place. In particular, calcium deficiency becomes common when the pH is wrong, and calcium is highly important. You will need to check your nutrient solution to determine the cause.

When the leaves curl down instead, there is the opposite problem—typically, there is too much fertilizing instead of not enough. You will want to then dilute down the nutrient solution to the recommended levels to ensure that the parameters are being met accordingly.

Plants Are Growing too Tall

When plants grow tall and skinny, it is usually a problem with the lighting. In particular, the plants will usually need more light when you find them growing like this. This is a huge problem—if your plants cannot get enough lighting, they are going to struggle later on. This is usually referred to as being "leggy." The natural solution, then, is to fix the lighting for your system to ensure that the plants are getting the right amount of light to ensure their own health.

This could also be a problem with temperature; however—you will want to take a look at the temperature in which you are growing. Is it a bit warmer than it is supposed to be? If so, you have an easy solution—you would simply lower the temperatures to ensure that everything grows as they are supposed to, allowing for more development in the right ways.

The Leaves Turn Purple After Flowering

Sometimes, after flowering, you may notice that your leaves begin to change color. They begin to turn purple instead, especially toward the end of the stage in which you can expect flowers. This can look quite concerning—but there is usually a pretty reasonable explanation for this. It is usually a problem with a deficiency in phosphorus. Flowers are quite demanding on phosphorus, and adjusting the nutrient solution and then providing the plant with a fresh nutrient solution is sometimes the easiest fix that can be employed.

You can also take a look at the temperature, especially during nighttime periods. Sometimes, that nighttime period temperature can get too cold, and that can cause problems.

The Flowers Are Rotting

Rotting flowers are the exact opposite of what you want to see when you are growing your own garden. It can be terrifying to see all of that hard work begin to wilt and fall off of your plant. Unfortunately, this is typically caused by a fungus that is not likely to be eliminated easily. When you see plants that have their flowers all dying off, usually, removing the plant and culling it from your system is the right answer to protect your garden and ensured that you do not run into those same problems again in the future. This will also prevent that infection from spreading further as well.

My Plant Isn't Growing

If you notice that your system does not seem to be growing much at all, there could be a common reason for it—it could be that your plants simply are not getting the right parameters that they need. When you realize that your yields seem small or when your plants are simply not growing much at all, it is crucial that you take a look at the parameters. Check temperature, lighting, and nutrient solution to ensure that everything looks optimized for the plants that you are growing.

The Roots Are Brown

Brown roots can be terrifying as well—it is usually a sign of something going dramatically wrong, and if your roots die, there is very little chance of saving the plant as well. When you notice that your roots are starting to look off, the best thing that you can do is take action. Brown, slimy roots are typically showing signs of root rot, especially if you can smell it on them. If you see that this is just beginning and you can still see signs of white roots, you may be able to save them, but if the entirety of your roots looks unhealthy, you may be better off culling the plant. However, if you do want to help treat the plants, you will need to foster regrowth. The dead roots will not heal—but they can be replaced. You will want to remove anything that is infected and then allow your plant to soak on its own to encourage regrowth.

Chapter 17: Starting Your Garden: Last Minute Skills You Need to Know

Now, before we head into looking at the profiles of the best plants that you can grow in your system, it is time to firstly take a look at three last skills that you need to master. These skills are, thankfully, quite simple, but any good gardener will need to have these tools in their arsenal. These skills are the ability to germinate your plant, to clone your plant, or to pollinate your plant. Germinating and cloning are the two most common ways that seeds and plants can be propagated without much of a struggle. They are great for ensuring that you can continue to grow new plants. Pollinating becomes a crucial skill when you are gardening in an area around which bees or other natural pollinators cannot reach on their own. Because of the lack of pollinators, you will sometimes have to play that role yourself.

Germinating Your Plants

Germinating starts with seeds. When you want to grow your garden through germination, you are deciding to grow your plants through the use of a seed, meaning that you are essentially creating a new plant for yourself. It will be genetically entirely unique—it will not have been taken from an already grown plant. Once germinated, the seed will become a sprout, a seedling, and then continue on throughout its cycle in peace. These plants can take a bit more time to grow, and sometimes, they will also require several years for the plants to mature properly in order to be productive in the first place. Nevertheless, germination is an incredibly important tool. Many plants will be just fine grown from germination, and some simply do better in this method. In particular, plants that do not repeatedly flower and produce new crops will almost always do better in germination. These are plants that are one harvest and done; for example—they rarely do well in the cloning process.

To germinate, you will have to do the following:

1. Gather your seeds and place them in a damp paper towel.

2. Put the damp paper towel somewhere dark and preferably warm.

3. Leave it for a few days.

4. Check on your plants. If the seeds have started to sprout, you will have succeeded.

There is another common method of germination in hydroponics that makes use of rockwool, creating an environment for your seeds to germinate within that will enable you to simply be able to transplant them without much of a problem. You will just be able to germinate and then place into your own system once they reach the seedling stage.

To do this, you will need to do the following:

1. Take several squares of rockwool—enough for one for every two or three seeds you intend to germinate. Always plant more than you expect to want or need—this ups your chances of success.

2. Balance the pH of the rockwool in water. Then, when it is ready, take it and, using a wooden skewer or toothpick, create a small hole in the rockwool's top. Place a seed into the rockwool and carefully place the wool back over itself with the tip of the skewer. Place two or three seeds in each square for optimization purposes. This ups the likelihood that you will grow plants.

3. Spray down the rockwool and keep it damp for the next several days. Place a glass bowl over the rockwool cubes so that you can trap the humidity and let the plants continue to grow. Spray daily.

4. When you see true leaves and roots, you can then transplant the rockwool directly into your system.

Cloning Your Plants

Cloning your plants has its own fair share of advantages as well. While you are certainly creating a plant that is genetically identical to the ones that you already had, there are certain advantages to doing so. In particular, you already know what to expect with the plants. You know what kind of fruit it tends to produce or how it tends to fare. You also will be able to avoid waiting for longer periods of time if your plant will need extra time for maturity. The clones of a mature plant are already mature—they just have to get to the right size before they can take advantage of that maturity first, meaning that all you are waiting for is the plant to get to the right size to produce.

Cloning is quite simple—all you have to do is take a snippet of a plant and allow it to root. The roots then are able to be transplanted into your own hydroponic system, saving you the time and the effort that would otherwise go into trying to germinate.

To clone your plants, you will follow these steps:

1. Choose a low-lying branch on a healthy plant. It should be a branch that is connected to the main stem, and it should be as close to the root structure as possible. The lower down on the plant that you go, the more likely it is that your plant will root.

2. Taking a pair of sterilized clippers or a sterile knife, make a cut along the stem without cutting into it at all.

You want to avoid damaging the main stem of the healthy plant. Then, trim the cutting that you created to be at a 45-degree angle. This will enable you to be able to better grow roots from the stem that has been clipped.

3. Prepare a square of rockwool—balance the pH and set it aside.

4. Take the trimming and begin to remove leaves. You want to cut off all leaves except for three or four right on the top. This will enable your plant to focus entirely on growing roots instead of spending all of its energy on photosynthesis. It will first prioritize the roots so that it can absorb the necessary nutrients to produce more leaves so it can grow.

5. (Optional) Take your plant and add a bit of rooting hormones to the tip of it. The hormones, while not required, do help the chances that your plant will root.

6. Place the rooting hormones into the rockwool and dampen it all. Keep it in a warm, sunny place and keep it damp until you begin to see roots sticking out of the square.

7. When you can see the roots, place it into your hydroponic system and let it grow.

Pollinating Your Plants

Finally, one last skill that you will be required to use in a hydroponic setting is that pollination. This is known as hand pollination. You will essentially be forcing the point—you will be transferring pollen from one plant to the next to create the fertilization process that you will need. Some plants are self-pollinators, meaning that every flower will have everything necessary to help them grow. All that has to happen is that wind will have to knock about the blossom enough to get the pollen to move. You can easily pollinate these. Other plants, however, have different blossoms with different parts. Some blossoms will have a stamen while others will have pistils. These are not self-pollinators—you will have to teach yourself to properly pollinate these plants to ensure they grow

The good news is that self-pollinating plants are quite easy to pollinate. All you need to do is gently run your hands back and forth across the blossoms. As you do this, you are essentially stirring up all of the pollen. You are moving it about and ensuring that it gets everywhere that it needs to go.

When your plants have distinct male and female flowers, you will need to remove the petals off of the male flowers so you can access the stamen. This is the part that is covered in pollen. Then, take a paintbrush and gently brush along the stamen to gather up the pollen onto the tip. You will then gently rub the brush into the center of the female blossoms, which will then complete the pollination process.

Chapter 18: Best Hydroponic Herbs for Beginners

No home kitchen is complete without its own herb garden, and luckily for you, you can begin to grow your own herbs to properly flavor and season your own meals, adding all sorts of great, fine flavors to be properly enjoyed. As you read through this chapter, you are going to be guided through four great herbs for beginners to grow in their own hydroponic gardens, along with the necessary parameters to ensure that they will properly grow.

You can grow herbs with other herbs, so long as their parameters line up enough to allow you to meet both needs at the same time. For example, basil and parsley would probably grow relatively well if kept together. This is a great way for you to ensure that you get the most out of your garden and can help when you are trying to figure out how to organize everything.

Oregano

Oregano is used commonly in many Mediterranean cuisines, especially in many Italian foods in particular. It can be dried out for future use or used as a fresh addition to your sauces and meats as well. It also grows very well in any hydroponic system.

- EC: 1.5-2.0

- pH: 6.0-8.0

- Temperature: 55-70 degrees Fahrenheit

- Lighting: 14 hours

Basil

Basil is great for any Italian food lover. Whether you enjoy copious amounts of pesto, or you simply want to have enough basil to go with tomatoes, this herb is a delicious one to add to your repertoire. This is one of the most common herbs to see in hydroponic settings. It is a warm herb, and it can be either germinated or produced through cloning cuttings. These plants should be regularly and readily trimmed down, which can commonly be a part of the harvesting process and allow you to better grow your plant and ensure that it is healthy. In general, which it will tolerate temperatures in the 60s, you want to aim for the high 70s or low 80s for a happy, healthy plant.

To properly grow and support this herb, you will want the following parameters:

- EC 1.6-2.2

- pH: 5.5-6.6

- Temperature: 65-95 degrees Fahrenheit

- Lighting: 10-12 hours a day

Parsley

Like basil, parsley is highly popular in the kitchen and is a very common garnish. These plants grow relatively readily, so long as you do provide them with everything that they will need. They grow most commonly in tower settings, but there is no reason that you could not grow this delicious herb in some of the simple methods that you were introduced to, such as the use of the glass jar Kratky or the plastic bottle wick methods. These plants are hardier to the cold than basil. They are also readily germinated and ready for harvest within a month.

- EC: .8-1.8

- pH: 5.5-6.0

- Temperature: 60-75 degrees Fahrenheit

- Lighting: Natural lighting is favored. Place it in a south-facing window and allow it to grow.

Cilantro

Cilantro is a widely popular herb, both in many Latin American dishes as well as many Asian ones. It is a great addition to any garden and is highly versatile. It typically requires higher levels of light, but if you can do this, you will have nearly endless cilantro—it grows rapidly in these higher levels of light, and care should be taken to not allow it to flower. If you see that it may begin to flower, you will want to cut it so it does not become bitter and ruin the taste. Cilantro is a bit odd in the fact that it not only likes high light, but it also prefers slightly lower temperatures to prevent bolting.

- EC: 1.6-1.8

- pH: 6.5-6.7

- Temperature 40-75 degrees Fahrenheit

- Lighting: 12 hours a day

Green Onion

Green onions are great plants to include in any hydroponic garden. They are commonly included as a garnish for many different cuisines, and some people even enjoy simply grilling them up and eating them on their own, enjoying the sweetness they develop. Keep in mind that green onions can be used in many ways, and you can even simply trim off the tops of the plants and allow the bases to keep growing a few times around to allow you to get more out of your crop. These plants may tolerate the cold, but they greatly prefer temperatures on the warmer sides and longer periods of time in the sunlight.

- EC: 1.8-2
- pH: 6-6.5
- Temperature: 68-77 Fahrenheit
- Lighting: 12-14 hours of light daily

Chives

Chives are closely related to green onions, but are slightly different. In particular, their bulbs are tiny, and they are tender, thin, and long, unlike green onions, which have larger bulbs and wider stalks. Chives are delicate and are great used as a sort of garnish. They also thrive in hydroponic settings, especially those such as the ebb and flow, where they are planted in the growing medium itself.

- EC: 1.8-2.4
- pH: 6.0-6.5
- Temperature: 65-80 degrees Fahrenheit
- Lighting: 14-16 hours daily

Dill

Delicate, yet distinctive, dill offers a common addition to many dips, sauces, and even pickles. It regularly is added to seafood, such as salmon, and it is also quite easy to grow as well. It can make a welcome addition to any garden, and it thrives in hydroponic settings.

- EC: 1.0-1.6
- pH: 5.5-6.4
- Temperature: 65-80 degrees Fahrenheit
- Lighting: 14 hours daily

Fennel

Fennel is a delicious herb that can be used to flavor eggs or delicate fish as well. It is entirely edible and you can harvest the greens as an herb or you can harvest the entirety of the plant to use the bulb as well. The bulbs are typically fully grown and ready to go when they are the side of a tennis ball.

- EC: 1.0-1.4
- pH: 6.4-6.8
- Temperature: 60-70 degrees Fahrenheit
- Lighting: 10 hours

Sage

Sage is a woody evergreen plant that can be grown year-round in your own hydroponic build. It thrives with the water and nutrients, and you are able to use this to flavor porks, poultry, and more to create delicious meals.

- EC: 1.0-1.6
- pH: 5.5-6.0

- Temperature: 75-85 degrees Fahrenheit
- Lighting: 12 hours daily

Chapter 19: Best Hydroponic Fruits for Beginners

Fruits themselves do not typically enjoy many of the hydroponic methods—or rather, they can pose quite the challenge for someone that does not quite know what he or she is doing. If you were to grow your own hydroponic fruits, there are a few different varieties that would be quite suited for beginners, but keep in mind that many of the options that you may see out there might be more difficult than you expected. This is because generally, fruiting plants will require several shifts in their nutrients to allow them to properly accommodate the different stages of growth. These particular fruits that you are going to be introduced to, however, are quite forgiving for beginners, and you should be able to make do with them quite well. As with the last chapter, you will be guided through understanding the fruit and the growing conditions.

Strawberries

Strawberries are perhaps some of the easiest plants to grow in a hydroponic system, despite the fact that they are fruiting. They thrive on the additional access to water, and they are commonly recommended for all beginners, and it helps greatly that they are so popular. If you wanted to grow a hydroponic garden and you liked strawberries at all, you should consider one of these plants. They can even be taught, indoors, to grow indefinitely. If you keep the parameters just right, you can ensure that they continue to produce, even in the winter.
These plants do best with an NFT, but you will also be able to grow them in other systems like an ebb and flow as well as the drip systems. However, if you were to try to grow them in a Kratky or a DWC, you might find that it is difficult. Keep in mind that strawberries are almost always better grown from

cuttings because they take two to three years before a new plant is ready to begin fruiting.

- EC: 1.4-3.0
- pH: 5.8-6.2

- Temperature: 60-80 degrees Fahrenheit

- Lighting 8-12 hours of light per day

Blueberries

Blueberries, despite being on bushes, are actually quite tolerant of the hydroponic growth cycle. They are quite able to thrive on NFT systems that will give them everything that they would need nutritionally, allowing for the constant production of berries once they do reach maturity. Keep in mind that most blueberries will not fruit for at least two years after germination. Keep in mind that these are bushes and as bushes, they are oftentimes a bit bigger, and you will need to be able to support them properly. However, they thrive in the low-pH conditions that you commonly see in hydroponic settings.

- EC 1.8-2.0

- pH: 4.5-5.8

- Temperature: 72-76 degrees Fahrenheit

- Lighting: 12-16 hours of light

Tomatoes

Tomatoes are another of those classic fruits that are perfect in a hydroponic setting. In fact, they usually thrive in them. They were actually the stars of the show when it came to first studying hydroponic growth, and because of their nearly unprecedented success with how well they grew, they are still commonly grown today in hydroponic settings. They are great in just about any system, and they do well so long as you are able to properly support the plants as they do develop, supporting them underneath the massive weights of themselves. These plants commonly grow well in trellised setups that will provide plenty of access to the plants as they fruit. Tomatoes are simple to grow at home and will work well in all of the methods that were provided, so long as you have a large enough container and you make it a point to ensure that your plants are provided within the right lighting and care.

- EC: 2.0-5.0

- pH: 5.5-6.5

- Temperature: 60-90 Fahrenheit

- Lighting: 12-16 hours

Watermelon

Despite the size, watermelons actually do great grown in a hydroponic setting, especially since they thrive on the constant access to water. If you or your family cannot get enough watermelon in the summer months cannot get enough watermelon, this is a great plant for you. The only real catch is that these plants tend to do the best in low-lying systems that will allow for the plant to not break its stems prematurely. It is possible to create sorts of supports if you were to use a hanging system, or you can make use of other methods as well, such as growing in a low-lying drip or NFT, allowing the plants to simply grow on the ground uninterrupted.

- EC: 1.5-2.4

- pH: 5.8

- Temperature: 70-90 degrees Fahrenheit

- Lighting: 10 hours per day

Bell Peppers

Botanically a fruit, bell peppers are another common pick for hydroponic systems. They are a bit more advanced than the other fruits offered, but they can still be grown relatively easily, especially with a DWC or ebb and flow system. With peppers, you want to avoid them growing to their full height—prune them back to about 8 inches and pinch them beyond that height to encourage pepper growth.

- EC: 2.0-2.5

- pH: 6.0-6.5

- Temperature: 65-75 degrees Fahrenheit

- Lighting: 18 hours of light per day, remembering to raise it as the plants grow higher

Cantaloupe

Despite what you might assume, cantaloupe is perfect for many different hydroponic builds. In fact, cantaloupe tends to thrive in a hydroponic crop. These parameters will hold true for just about any muskmelon, the family in which cantaloupe belongs. Keep in mind that you will want to ensure that your vines and fruit have plenty of space for themselves to be supported and make sure that you meet their needs. Keep in mind that these plants require higher levels of potassium and limit the fruit per plant to just 3 or 4 to ensure high quality fruit.

- EC: 2.2-2.6

- pH: 6.5-7.0

- Temperature: 72-90 degrees Fahrenheit

- Lighting: 16 hours per day

Chapter 20: Best Hydroponic Vegetables for Beginners

Finally, we are going to take a look at a handful of vegetables that commonly thrive in any hydroponic system. There are vegetables that are likely to be commonly used in any kitchen as well—meaning, if you could grow these vegetables for yourself, you would eliminate the need to purchase these vegetables from the store, instead enjoying the fresher, home-grown produce that you can make yourself. As you read through this chapter, you will be guided through beginner's vegetables, and this is by no means a comprehensive list of what can be grown. If there is a vegetable that was not on this list that you would like to see grown hydroponically, there is a good chance that you can find all of the essential information to do just that online.

Lettuce

Lettuce is highly versatile. From using it in salads to making sandwiches or tacos with it, lettuce can be used in just about any cuisine around the world. It is a great palate cleanser and adds a nice, crisp, refreshing bite to many different meals. If you do decide to grow lettuce, you are best served growing loose leaf varieties as opposed to the ones that tend to wrap around themselves in heads. While you can grow these methods at home, too, they typically do not yield such large harvests, and if you want that larger payoff, you will want the lettuce with a loose leaf.

If you do want to grow lettuce, you can do so in any of the methods that were shown to you in this book. Lettuce will grow equally well in all of these without much light at all. So long as the nutrient solution is ready and the plants themselves have enough space to grow, they will, and you will get to enjoy the lettuce to yourself. Keep in mind that you can even just harvest the outer leaves when you do decide to harvest—this will keep it growing longer and bring you more harvests over time. Also, keep in mind that too much light or too high of temperatures will lead to your plant bolting, meaning that it will start flowering, and that will lead to very bitter taste.

- EC: 1.4

- pH: 5.5-6.0

- Temperature: 50-70 degrees Fahrenheit

- Lighting: 10-14 hours in low or moderate light. They do just fine with CFL.

Spinach

Spinach is another highly popular leafy green that can be grown with ease in a hydroponic setting. You will simply need to provide your garden with everything that it will need to thrive, and you will find that you are highly successful in ensuring that it will develop properly. It can be cared for simply, and so long as you make sure that you keep the temperature low at temperatures that the lettuce can tolerate, it should grow just fine. Like lettuce, spinach does best germinated rather than grown from a clipping thanks to the way that it grows. Also, like lettuce, your spinach will bolt if you keep the temperature too high.

- EC: 1.8-2.3

- pH: 5.5-6.6

- Temperature: 60-70 degrees Fahrenheit

- Lighting: Low light—it prefers less intense lighting. Direct light or intense light is too much, and it will not thrive. It needs 12 hours daily—preferably fluorescent or HID, but at a distance.

Beans

Beans of all kinds, while technically a legume, are going to be included with the other vegetables in this book. All types of beans are quite simple to grow, and they tend to thrive well in a hydroponic system. They usually germinate quickly and then begin to sprout rapidly. They will grow in just about any system that you set up, regardless of what it is, but they do prefer ebb and flow over the others. If you cannot make that happen, however, do not worry and do not get discouraged. You can grow them still! All you have to do is make sure that you are going to provide them with the right environment.

- EC: 2-4

- pH 6-6.5

- Temperature: 70-80 degrees Fahrenheit, lower at night and higher during the day

- Lighting: Full sunlight—12-13 hours per day. They NEED a night cycle of at least 10 hours, but preferably more like 12 to grow optimally.

Broccoli

Broccoli is yet another great, easy vegetable that will thrive in a hydroponic setting. If you want to feed your family something that you know will nourish them and get them to enjoy the fruits (or vegetables!) of your labor, broccoli is a great one to add to the mix. As a cool-weather crop, it is quite simple to manage in just about any setting, and it will grow well in all of the different growing methods, so long as you make sure that it has enough space. Just try to avoid NFT as they typically do not have large enough pipes, unless you custom-made your own system just for broccoli.

- EC: 2.8-3.5
- pH: 5.5-6.5
- Temperature: 55-65 degrees Fahrenheit
- Lighting: 14-16 hours per day of low-heat light—preferably CFL or LED. HID tends to heat it up too much.

Cauliflower

Cauliflower, like broccoli, is quite simple to grow in a hydroponic system. They provide a great side vegetable to use in meals and they are quite nutritious as well.

- EC: 0.5-2
- pH: 6.0-7.0
- Temperature: 55-70 degrees Fahrenheit
- Lighting: 14+ hours

Kale

Kale can be a great way for you to add some extra calcium into your diet and ensure that what you are eating is healthy. It is also quite readily grown in a hydroponic setting, and you will be able to make great use out of nearly any hydroponic build if you want this.

- EC: 1.0-2.3

- pH: 5.5-6.5

- Temperature: 40-65 degrees Fahrenheit

- Lighting: 10+ hours per day of low-heat light

Bok Choy

Bok choy is another leafy green that thrives in hydroponic settings. It is a Chinese cabbage that is winter hardy and it can be a great source of all sorts of vitamins, being particularly dense in many of the vitamins and minerals that you need.

- EC: 1.5-2.5

- pH: 6.0-7.0

- Temperature: 50-70 degrees Fahrenheit

- Lighting: 7+ hours daily

Onions

Onions are incredibly versatile in cooking and are commonly used in most dishes as a way to add flavor. From adding a slice to sandwiches to sautéing them, or even roasting them with your meat, onions are readily used to make food taste better. Despite commonly growing in the soil, you can grow them hydroponically as well.

- EC: 1.8-2.2

- pH: 6.0-7.0

- Temperature: 65-70 degrees Fahrenheit

- Lighting: 12 hours daily

Carrots

Like onions, carrots commonly do quite well in hydroponic settings. All you have to do is make sure that you provide them with the proper nutrients that they will need. Keep in mind that for carrots, the roots should not be fully submerged—they would do best with an ebb and flow system.

- EC: 1.4-2.2
- pH: 6.0-6.5
- Temperature: 50-85 degrees Fahrenheit
- Lighting: 6-12 hours daily

Conclusion

And with that, we have made it to the end of this book! Hopefully, at this point, you are beginning to feel convinced that hydroponics is the right method for you. With all of its benefits, how could it not be? It can be grown in just about any setting and any space allotment. You can use any lighting, ranging from sunlight to making use of even fluorescent bulbs. It is an affordable indoor option for just about anyone, and you can even make builds with items that you can probably find in your home right this moment. Now, let's recap…

Hydroponics is the art of growing without soil. You can grow your plants with ease without ever having to get dirty, get down to weed, or having to water your plants twice a day. You do not have to plant them outdoors, and you are not constrained by the climate in which you live. This is greatly beneficial. No matter where you live right now, no matter what time of year it is while you are reading this book, you can start your own garden. Even if there is a pile of snow outside your window, you can begin to grow your own hydroponic garden, and it could not be easier.

While hydroponic gardening may sound difficult at first, remember, it is actually quite doable. It may be full of big words like "germination," or fancy names for the systems, but they are all quite manageable for anyone! No matter whether you have never gardened before in your life or if you are simply trying to branch away from traditional gardening into something that is a bit more accessible to you, or to try something new, this type of gardening is a great starting point.

With practice, you could even begin to grow significant amounts of your family's food with your own two hands. You could turn an unfinished basement into a year-round utopia, filled up with all sorts of goodies and freshly grown produce for your family's enjoyment! All you would have to do is take the time to build the setup for it.

Who knows, if you got efficient at gardening, you could even begin to start up your own business venture providing locally sourced produce to your town—that is not outside of the realm of possibility! These gardens are highly versatile, and they can be scaled up and down with ease. All that really matters is that you are willing and able to spend the time and energy to get it going and to take care of it yourself. If you want to garden for your town, you have the power to do that. It is not nearly as difficult to get started as you may think, and if you have made it this far into the book, you have already taken a monumental first step! All that is left is to put it to work and make it happen yourself.

From here, start thinking. What are your long-term goals? Do you want to grow your own farm? Or just produce for your family? Maybe you just want to start small, and that is okay, too! No matter what your goals, this book is here for you as a reference. This book is here if you need something to fall back on. This book will help you through the beginning steps of the gardening process, if you are willing to have it.

Congratulations!

Now you know everything about Hydroponics Gardening

If you loved reading this book, please let me know your thoughts by leaving a review on Amazon, I would really appreciate that

Thank you!

Printed in Great Britain
by Amazon